Lionel Carley

London

7 February 1984

A REGISTER OF
FIRST PERFORMANCES
OF
ENGLISH OPERAS

A Register of First Performances of English Operas and Semi-Operas
from the 16th Century to 1980

compiled by

ERIC WALTER WHITE

The Society for Theatre Research

1983

Published by The Society for Theatre Research
77 Kinnerton Street, London SW1X 8ED

ISBN 0 85430 036 8

Text set in 9/10 pt Linotron 202 Times, printed and bound
in Great Britain at The Pitman Press, Bath

Foreword

'Operas abroad are plays where every word is sung; this is not relished in England.' These words by a writer in *The Gentleman's Journal* for 1693 may at one time have summed up the average Englishman's opinion, but in fact the English theatre by the end of the seventeenth century had, in the words of the late Alfred Loewenberg, achieved some very original English solutions of the operatic problem. The Elizabethan farce jigs, the Jacobean court masques, works with texts by William Davenant and with music by John Blow and Henry Purcell had laid what might have been the foundations of a native school of opera.

That this root failed to flower was an accident of history, due to the fashionable popularity of Italian opera in the eighteenth century and to the overpowering influence of the great Italian and German masters in the nineteenth. Nevertheless, there were far from insignificant contributions from Britain in the works of Thomas Arne and Charles Dibdin, in the brief but glorious flowering of ballad opera, and in the quintessentially English partnership of Gilbert and Sullivan, as well as in the works of a host of less familiar composers which do not deserve to be forgotten. In the twentieth century Ralph Vaughan Williams and Gustav Holst made significant contributions to an English style of opera, and within our lifetime the works of Benjamin Britten, William Walton and Michael Tippett, with their many successors, have, rightly, received international recognition.

In the light of all this, it is to be hoped that a work listing the first performance of English operas will make a contribution towards the appreciation of a native art form that has, in the past, often been under-estimated or ignored.

This Register was originally planned as an Appendix to my *History of English Opera* (Faber & Faber 1983). I am grateful to The Society for Theatre Research, whose active interest has enabled this Register to appear contemporaneously with the main historical work. It is hoped that it will stand alone as a work of reference in its own right.

The list is selective, and includes only works that have been publicly performed. An English opera has generally been taken to mean a stage action with vocal and instrumental music written by a British composer to an English libretto. Owing to insuperable problems of definition the list has been extended to include works that might be described as 'semi-operas': masques which include a reasonable proportion of vocal music, farce jigs, pasticcios, burlettas, as well as dramatic operas, operettas, and other forms of operatic entertainment. When the description of a work, *e.g.* 'masque', 'dramatic opera', etc. is given within inverted commas, this means that the work was so designated on the title page of its score or libretto.

On the other hand, it has been impossible to include every work containing some musical element. Many pieces described as comic operas, dramatic operas, musical extravaganzas, and so on have been judged as possessing insufficient musical importance to be listed here; they can be identified in Allardyce Nicoll's *History of English Drama*, in connection with which the article by George Hauger on 'English Musical Theatre 1830–1900' in *Theatre Notebook* xxxvi 2 and 3 (1982), contains a number of valuable additions and corrections. Similarly, operas performed on puppet stages have not been included, as they are already listed in George Speaight's *History of the English Puppet Theatre*. And finally, no attempt has been made to list the musical comedies and musicals of the twentieth century, as these constitute a distinct art form that deserves its own separate treatment; in so far as much of this has been American-inspired, Gerald Bordman's *American Musical Theatre: A Chronicle* provides a comprehensive guide.

Names of composers and librettists are given when known. In the case of court masques, the designer played such an important part that whenever possible his name is given too. Details of translations are given only where first performances have been in a foreign language. Operas in which there is no spoken dialogue are marked with an asterisk*.

Where the theatre of production is an opera-house and no specific mention is made of a presenting company, the home company should be understood. It will be appreciated that many English operas have received *ad hoc* productions, particularly in the twentieth century. With some of the earlier entries, an attempt has been made to indicate where the music, if extant, can be found.

Where an opera or semi-opera does not conform to these general rules, but still seems worthy of special mention in the context of English opera generally (*e.g.* Weber's *Oberon*), the entry is given within square brackets.

E. W. W.

A Register of First Performances of English Operas and Semi-Operas

1517 or somewhat later ANON: *The Four Elements*
'Interlude'. Text by John Rastell. One scene.
There are five cues for music. The music for the song 'Tyme to pas with goodly sport' is printed in the libretto. The same music (set to different words) is found in a manuscript music book of about 1515, which has been published as volume XVIII of *Musica Britannica*, 'Music at the Court of King Henry VIII'. It is probable that the other music was also adapted from already existing material.

c. **1564** RICHARD EDWARDS: *Damon and Pithias*
There are several musical numbers for the characters in this 'excellent Comedie of two the moste faithfullest Freendes'. Text by Richard Edwards, Master of the Children of the Chapel Royal. The first performance was given before Elizabeth I and her Court at Whitehall, Christmas 1564. The music has not survived.

1584 ANON: *The Arraignment of Paris*
6 January. Whitehall
'Pastoral'. Text by George Peele. Five acts. Performed by the Children of the Chapel. The music is lost.

Before 1590 ANON: *Rowland**
Farce jig. Text by William Kemp. One scene.
The English text of this earliest of farce jigs has been lost; but various German translations are extant, the earliest of which was published in 1599. There is a strong supposition that this popular jig had a sequel, for the Stationers' Register contains the entry 'the Seconde parte of the gigge betwene Rowland and the Sexton' dated 16 December 1581. It is thought Kemp may have taken *Rowland* with him when he went abroad to the Low Countries in 1585 and Denmark in 1586. The jig has four characters and was sung to one tune, which appears in *Lady Neville's Book* (1591) as 'Lord Willobies Welcome Home' and in the *Fitzwilliam Book* as 'Rowland'.
A new arrangement of this jig made by Anthony Bernard, with the English text reconstructed by John Barton from the contemporary German translation, was broadcast by the B.B.C. on its Third Programme on 9 September 1957.

c. **1590** ANON: *[The Wooing of Nan*]*
Farce jig. Text by Christopher Marlowe(?). One scene.
This dialogue is to be found in a late 16th century manuscript belonging to Dulwich College. There is no title; but it is usually referred to as *The Wooing of Nan*. On the blank verso of the leaf on which it is written, the words 'Kitt Marlowe' have been written in a different and later hand. Though Marlowe may not have been the author, external and internal evidence points to a date round about 1590, when it could have been performed by the Admiral's Men as an afterpiece to one of Marlowe's plays. It was sung to two tunes, neither of which is specified.

1

ANON: *Rowland's Godson**
Farce jig. Text by William Kemp(?). One scene.
On 18 and 29 April 1592 the two parts of 'Rowlandes godson moralized'
were entered in the Stationers' Register to John Wolfe. The date of
composition is likely to have been a year or two earlier. There is a
reference to this farce jig in the Induction of Nashe's *Summer's Last Will
and Testament*, probably written in 1592. The jig was sung to one tune,
'Loth to depart'.

c. **1591**   **ANON:** *The Hunting of Cupid*
'Pastoral'. Text by George Peele.
On 26 July 1591 *The Hunting of Cupid* was entered in the Registers of the
Stationers' Company. It is likely that the play was published; but no copy
is known to have survived, nor is there any record of a performance.

1595   **ANON:** *[Masque of Proteus]*
3 or 4 March. Whitehall
Masque, produced by the gentlemen of Gray's Inn. Text by Francis
Davison. One act.[1] The music has not survived. The text was published
in *Gesta Grayorum*, London, 1688.

ANON: *Attowell's Jig**
Farce jig. Text by George Attowell. One scene.
This was licensed to Thomas Gosson on 14 October 1595 as 'A pretie
newe Jigge betwene ffrancis the gentleman Richard the farmer and their
wyves'. The tunes are specified: 'Walsingham', 'the Iewish dance', 'Bugle
Boe', 'goe from my window'.

ANON: *Singing Simpkin**
Farce jig. Text by Richard Tarlton(?). One scene.
The date of this jig is probably fixed by the entry to Thomas Gosson on 21
October 1595 of 'a ballad called Kemps *newe Jygge* betwixt a souldiour
and a Miser and Sym the clown'. Richard Tarlton may have performed or
even written it. Kemp certainly played in it. It was sung to two tunes,
which are not named in the printed text.[2] Its vogue in England and on
the continent lasted for a century. According to the second edition of
Actaeon and Diana, it was 'acted at the Red Bull with great applause'.

1602   **ANON:** *[Michael and Frances*]*
Christmas. Osmotherly, Yorkshire
Farce jig. Text by Francis Mitchell. One scene.
The title of this jig, which is untitled in the original manuscript, is due to
C. J. Sisson, who in *Lost Plays of Shakespeare's Age* showed that after
various amateur performances it was first given professionally, probably
by the Egton Players, at Christmas 1602. All six tunes are specified, *viz.*
'ffiliday fflouts mee', 'ffortune', 'take thy old Cloake about thee', 'the
Ladies of Essex Lamentacon', 'ffor her Aperne', 'the Cobler'.

---

(1) In the case of masques, the designation 'act' is used to imply a continuous
action, with or without scenic changes or transformations.
(2) Robert Cox, *Actaeon and Diana*, first edition n.d.; second edition 1656.

A new arrangement of this jig, with the original tunes edited by Elizabeth Poston, was performed at Hampton Court Palace on 23 July 1951.

1604   ANON: *The Vision of the Twelve Goddesses*
8 January. Hampton Court Palace, Great Hall Queen's masque. Text by Samuel Daniel. One act. Presented by the Queen's Majesty and her Ladies. The music has not survived.

1605   ALFONSO FERRABOSCO:[1] The Masque of Blackness
6 January. Whitehall, Banqueting House
Queen's masque. Text by Ben Jonson.[2] Descriptions by Inigo Jones. One act. One number was printed in *Ayres* by Alfonso Ferrabosco, 1609.

ANON: *Alba*
27 August. Oxford, Christ Church Hall
The text of this pastoral, which was probably in Latin, has been lost, and the music has not survived. From the description of the characters, their costumes, and the 'many rusticall songes and dances', it sounds as if it resembled a masque. It was performed before James I, Queen Anne, and the Princes Henry and Charles.[3]

1606   A. FERRABOSCO: *Hymenaei, or, The Solemnities of Mask and Barriers*
5 January. Whitehall, Banqueting House
Court masque to celebrate the marriage of Robert, Earl of Essex, with Lady Frances Howard, second daughter of the Earl of Suffolk. Text by Ben Jonson. Decorations by Inigo Jones. One act.

1607   THOMAS CAMPION, THOMAS GILES, THOMAS LUPO: *[Masque in Honour of the Lord Hayes and his Bride]*
6 January. Whitehall, Banqueting House[4]
Court masque. Text by Thomas Campion. One act. Some of the music was published (1607) and some has survived in various manuscript collections, particularly British Library. Add. MS 10444.

1608   A. FERRABOSCO: *The Masque of Beauty*
10 January. Whitehall, Banqueting House[5]

(1) In the case of masques it is always possible that musicians other than those actually named here may have supplied or adapted some of the music.
(2) Ben Jonson had already supplied the text for *Satyr, or, The Masque of Fairies*, an open-air entertainment offered to Queen Anne of Denmark at Althorp in Northamptonshire on 25 June 1603 during her progress south from Edinburgh to London at the time of the accession of her husband James VI of Scotland to the throne of England.
(3) An account of the occasion by Philip Stringer can be found in British Museum MS Harl. 7044 and is printed in J. Nichols, *The Progresses of King James I*, London, 1828.
(4) The room in which this masque was given is described in the libretto as 'the great Hall'.
(5) A new Banqueting House, constructed of brick and stone, was inaugurated with this masque.

Queen's masque. Text by Ben Jonson. One act. Several numbers were printed in *Ayres* by Alfonso Ferrabosco, 1609.

A. FERRABOSCO: *Masque at the Marriage of Viscount Haddington*[1]
9 February. Whitehall, Banqueting House
Court masque. Text by Ben Jonson. One act. One number was printed in *Ayres* by Alfonso Ferrabosco, 1609.

1609 A. FERRABOSCO: *The Masque of Queens*
2 February. Whitehall, Banqueting House
Queen's masque. Text by Ben Jonson. Decorations by Inigo Jones. One act. The first masque to feature an antimasque (*sic*). One number was printed in *Ayres* of Alfonso Ferrabosco, 1609.

1610 ANON: *Tethys' Festival, or, the Queen's Wake*
5 June. Whitehall, Banqueting House
Masque. Text by Samuel Daniel. Decorations by Inigo Jones. One act.

1611 A. FERRABOSCO and ROBERT JOHNSON: *Oberon, the Fairy Prince*
1 January. Whitehall, Banqueting House
Prince Henry's masque. Text by Ben Jonson. Decorations by Inigo Jones. One act. Some of the music has survived.
  The satyrs' dance was incorporated into Shakespeare's *The Winter's Tale*.

A. FERRABOSCO: *Love Freed from Ignorance and Folly*
3 February. Whitehall, Banqueting House
Queen's masque. Text by Ben Jonson. One act. Some of the music has survived.

1612 ANON: *Love Restored*
6 January. Whitehall
Court masque. Text by Ben Jonson. One act.

1613 T. CAMPION and OTHERS: *The Lords' Masque*
14 February. Whitehall, Banqueting House
Court masque. Text by Thomas Campion. Decorations by Inigo Jones. One act.
  Written for the marriage of Princess Elizabeth to the Count Palatine. One of Campion's songs was printed with the music for the Masque at the Marriage of the Earl of Somerset (1614).

ANON: *The Masque of the Middle Temple and Lincoln's Inn*
15 February. Whitehall, Banqueting House.

---

(1) The full title of the libretto is 'The Description of the Masque with the Nuptial Songs at the Lord Viscount Haddington's Marriage at Court on the Shrove-Tuesday at Night, 1608'.

Masque, presented by the gentlemen of the Middle Temple and Lincoln's Inn. Text by George Chapman. Decorations by Inigo Jones. One act.

JOHN COPRARIO: *The Masque of the Inner Temple and Gray's Inn*
20 February. Whitehall, Banqueting House
Court masque, presented by the gentlemen of the Inner Temple and Gray's Inn. Text by Francis Beaumont. One act. Some of the music has survived.

The second antimasque was utilised in Fletcher and Shakespeare's *The Two Noble Kinsmen*.

J. COPRARIO and NICHOLAS LANIER: *Masque at the Marriage of the Earl of Somerset and the Lady Frances Howard*[1]
26 December. Whitehall, Banqueting House
King's masque. Text by Thomas Campion. One act. Four of the songs were published (1614).

ANON: *The Irish Masque*
29 December. Whitehall, Banqueting House
Court masque. Text by Ben Jonson. One act.

1614 J. COPRARIO:[2] *The Masque of Flowers*
6 January. Whitehall, Banqueting House
Masque, presented by the gentlemen of Gray's Inn. Text anonymous.[3] One act. Some of the music has survived.

1615 ANON: *The Golden Age Restored*
6 January. Whitehall, Banqueting House
Court masque. Text by Ben Jonson. One act.

ANON: *[Ulysses and Circe]*
13 January. Inner Temple
Masque, presented by the gentlemen of the Inner Temple. Text by William Browne. Three scenes.[4]

1616 ANON: *Mercury Vindicated from the Alchemists*
1 January. Whitehall, Banqueting House
Court masque. Text by Ben Jonson. One act.

ANON: *Christmas his Mask*
December. Whitehall, Banqueting House
Court masque. Text by Ben Jonson. One act.

(1) Sometimes known as *Somerset's Masque* and *The Squires' Masque*.
(2) It appears likely that Nicholas Lanier and John Wilson collaborated over the music.
(3) The dedication of the libretto to Sir Francis Bacon is signed with the initials 'I.G. W.D. T.B.' But Bacon himself may have been implicated in the authorship.
(4) These three scenes are specified in the libretto.

1617   ANON: *The Vision of Delight*
6 January. Whitehall, Banqueting House
Court masque. Text by Ben Jonson. One act. 'Delight spake in song, *Stylo recitativo.*'

N. LANIER: *Lovers Made Men**
22 February. Blackfriars[1]
Masque, presented by friends of Lord Hay. Text by Ben Jonson. One act. The opening stage direction includes the statement that '*the whole Masque was sung after the Italian manner*, stilo recitativo, *by Master Nicholas Lanier, who ordered and made both the Scene and the music.*' The music has not survived.
   In 1963 Andrew J. Sabol published a score (Brown University Press) constructed from other music by Lanier and his contemporaries.

ANON: *Cupid's Banishment*
May. Deptford, Greenwich
Masque. Text by Robert White.[2] Written 'for younge Gentlewomen of the Ladies' Hall in Deptford at Greenwich' and presented before the Queen.

1618   ANON: *Pleasure Reconciled to Virtue*
6 January. Whitehall, Banqueting House
Prince's masque. Text by Ben Jonson. Decorations by Inigo Jones. One act.
   The Comus antimasque here is very similar to the Bacchus antimasque in *Cupid's Banishment* (1617).

ANON: *For the Honour of Wales*
17 February. Whitehall, Banqueting House
Court masque. Text by Ben Jonson. One act. (Performed with the main masque of *Pleasure Reconciled to Virtue*.)

1619   ANON: *Masque of Heroes*
January. Inner Temple
Masque, presented by the gentlemen of the Inner Temple together with five actors from Prince Charles's Men. Text by Thomas Middleton. One act.

1620   ANON: *News from the New World Discovered in the Moon*
17 January. Whitehall[3]
Court masque, preceded by a scene of low comedy. Text by Ben Jonson. One act.

ANON: *Pan's Anniversary, or, The Shepherds' Holiday*
19 June. Greenwich Palace

(1) At the Wardrobe, of which Lord Hay was Master.
(2) Printed in J. Nichols, *The Progresses of King James I*, London, 1828, from a manuscript owned by William Upcott, which appears to have been subsequently lost.
(3) This masque was staged somewhere in Whitehall, but not in the old Banqueting House, which had been destroyed by fire the previous year.

Court masque. Text by Ben Jonson. Decorations by Inigo Jones. One act. Performed on James I's birthday.

1621 ANON: *Fool's Fortune**
Summer. Claverly, Shropshire
Farce jig. Author of the text unknown. One scene.
     Like *Michael and Frances* (1602), the text of this jig was discovered by C. J. Sisson. Four tunes are specified—'A:B:C'; 'barnaby'; 'Jockey there man'; 'new masque'.

ROBERT JOHNSON: *The Gypsies Metamorphosed*
3 August. Burley-on-the-Hill
Masque, Text by Ben Jonson. One act.
This masque was performed thrice before James I—at Burley-on-the-Hill, the estate of the Marquis of Buckingham (3 August); at Belvoir, the estate of the Earl of Rutland (5 August); and at Windsor (some time in September).
     Some of the songs are in a manuscript volume of dramatic songs in the Bodleian, Oxford.

1622 A. FERRABOSCO and N. LANIER: *The Masque of Augurs*
6 January. Whitehall, Banqueting House[1]
Court masque, preceded by a scene of low comedy. Text by Ben Jonson. Decorations by Inigo Jones. One act.

1623 ANON: *Time Vindicated to Himself and to his Honours*
19 January. Whitehall, Banqueting House
Court masque. Text by Ben Jonson. Decorations by Inigo Jones. One act.

1624 [ANON: *Neptune's Triumph for the Return of Albion*
This one-act court masque, with text by Ben Jonson, was prepared for 6 January 1624; but its performance was cancelled because of a dispute over precedence between the French and Spanish Ambassadors. See *The Fortunate Isles* (1625).]

1625 ANON: *The Fortunate Isles, and their Union*
9 January. Whitehall, Banqueting House
Court masque. Text by Ben Jonson. Decorations by Inigo Jones. One act.
This masque included material from *Neptune's Triumph for the Return of Albion* (1624).

Before 1626 ANON: *Simon and Susan**
This is a wooing dialogue rather than a farce jig; but as it has four characters, two of whom (Susan's parents) have separate entries, its inclusion here would seem to be justified. It was sung to a single tune, 'I can, nor will no longer lye alone'. The terminal date for its performance is derived from the fact that there were two published editions, one printed by Henry Gosson who was active between 1603 and 1641, and the other

(1) This was the first Court masque to be staged in Inigo Jones's new Banqueting House.

by 'W.I.', probably one of two printers named William Jones, who were active between 1589 and 1618, and between 1601 and 1626 respectively.

c. **1630**   HENRY LAWES: *Arcades*
Harefield House, Middlesex
Text by John Milton. One scene. Described in the Trinity manuscript of Milton's minor poems[1] as 'part of a maske'; but this was corrected by Milton to 'part of an entertainment'. First performed for Alice Countess Dowager of Derby, stepmother of the Earl of Bridgewater. Some scholars have suggested 1633 as a probable date; but the earlier date seems more likely. The music (to the three songs) has not survived.

1631   ANON: *Love's Triumph through Callipolis**
9 January. Whitehall, Banqueting House
King's masque. Text by Ben Jonson. Decorations by Inigo Jones. One act.

ANON: *Chloridia, Rites to Chloris and her Nymphs*
22 February. Whitehall, Banqueting House
Queen's masque. Text by Ben Jonson. Decorations by Inigo Jones. One act. The last masque on which Jonson and Jones worked together.

1632   ANON: *Albion's Triumph*
8 January. Whitehall, Banqueting House
King's masque. Text by Aurelian Townshend. Decorations by Inigo Jones. One act.

ANON: *Tempe Restored*
14 February. Whitehall, Banqueting House
Queen's masque. Text by Aurelian Townshend. Decorations by Inigo Jones. One act. An adaptation of Beaujoyleux's *Balet Comique de la Royne* (1582).

Before   ANON: *The Black Man*
1633   Farce jig. Date and place of first performance unknown. Text by Robert Cox. One scene.
    This jig was first printed by Francis Kirkman in a collection of skits entitled *The Wits, or, Sport upon Sport* (1673). In the preface, Robert Cox, who was closely connected with the Red Bull Theatre, is mentioned as principal actor and contriver. The eight tunes are not specified. The jig contains prose passages that were spoken.
    A performing version was made by David King and produced at the Arts Theatre, Cambridge, on 11 March 1952.

1634   WILLIAM LAWES, SIMON IVES and DAVIS MELL:
The Triumph of Peace
3 February. Whitehall, Banqueting House
Masque, presented by the gentlemen of the four Inns of Court. Text by James Shirley. Five scenes.
    One of the most expensive masques ever produced. Its cost was said to be £21,000. Some of William Lawes's music has survived.[2]

(1) A facsimile of the manuscript in Trinity College, Cambridge, was published by the Scolar Press, Ilkley, in 1970.
(2) Bodleian Mus. Sch. B. 2; British Library Add. MS. 31432; and Edinburgh University, Ms. Dc. 1.69, fol 109(8).

At the Queen's express request, the masque was repeated; and by invitation of the Lord Mayor of London, this repetition was held at the Merchant Taylors' Hall in the City on 13 February 1634.

H. LAWES: *Coelum Britannicum*
18 February. Whitehall, Banqueting House
King's masque. Text by Thomas Carew.[1] Decorations by Inigo Jones. One act.

H. LAWES: *Comus*
29 September (Michaelmas Day). Ludlow Castle, Shropshire Masque. Text by J. Milton. One act. The masque was presented before the Earl of Bridgewater, then President of Wales.
   H. Lawes's setting of the five songs is to be found in the Lawes Manuscript acquired by the British Library in 1966 (Add. MS. 53723). An early draft of the text is included in the Trinity manuscript of Milton's minor poems—see *Arcades* (*c.* 1630) above.

[ANON: *Love's Mistresse, or, The Queens Masque*
November. Phoenix, Drury Lane
Text by Thomas Heywood. Five acts.
   This is a play with incidental music rather than a masque. Its first public performance at the Phoenix Theatre, with the King and Queen present, was followed within the space of eight days by two other performances at Denmark House in the Strand, the first of which took place on 19 November, the thirty-fourth birthday of Charles I. According to the prologue specially written for that occasion, henceforward the play was to bear the title of the Queen's Masque. The composer of the music, which consists mainly of dances and a few songs, is not known. Inigo Jones devised the scenes and machines for the Denmark House production.]

1635   ANON: *The Temple of Love*
10 February. Whitehall, Banqueting House
Queen's masque. Text by William Davenant. Decorations by Inigo Jones. One act.
   'This masque . . . for the newness of the invention, variety of Scaenes, Apparitions, and richness of habits was generally approved to be one of the most magnificent that hath been done in *England*.'

1636   HENRY and WILLIAM LAWES: *The Triumphs of the Prince D'Amour**
24 February. Middle Temple
Masque, presented by the gentlemen of the Middle Temple. Text by W. Davenant. Decorations by M. Corseilles. One act. Some of the music is extant.[2]

---

(1) When this masque was first printed in 1634, the author's name was given as Thomas Carew; but, for some reason or other, its text was included in the folio edition of William Davenant's Collected Works (1673).
(2) Bodleian, Mus. Sch. B2. One song by William Lawes was printed by John Playford in *Select Ayres and Dialogues* (1669). This masque was through-composed; but unlike *Lovers Made Man* (1617) it contained no recitative.

[HENRY LAWES and OTHERS: *The Royal Slave*
30 August. Oxford, Christ Church Hall
Text by William Cartwright. This entertainment was described as a play;
but it contained music and dancing. Settings by Henry Lawes of 'Com
from the Dungeon to the Throne' are to be found in the British Library
(Add. MS. 29396 and Add. MS. 53723. After its first performance at
Oxford, this entertainment was repeated at Hampton Court.]

1638 WILLIAM LAWES: *Britannia Triumphans*
7 January. Whitehall, Masquing House
King's masque. Text by W. Davenant. Decorations by Inigo Jones. One
act. A considerable amount of the music has survived.[1]

ANON[2]: *Luminalia, or, The Festival of Light*
6 February. Whitehall, Masquing House
Queen's masque. Text by W. Davenant. Decorations by Inigo Jones. One
act.

1640 LOUIS RICHARD: *Salmacida Spolia*
21 January. Whitehall, Masquing House
Their Majesties' masque. Text by W. Davenant. Decorations by Inigo
Jones and John Webb. One act.
   'This Masque . . . was generally approved of, especially by all strangers
that were present, to be the noblest and most ingenuous [sic] that hath
been done here in that kind.'

1653 CHRISTOPHER GIBBONS and MATTHEW LOCKE:
Cupid and Death
26 March. Private entertainment in London
Masque. Text by James Shirley. One act (three scenes)
   The performance which Luke Channen (or Channell as he is referred to
by Pepys) organised on 26 March 1653 was attended by the Portuguese
Ambassador. Channen was a dancing master; and it seems likely that this
masque may have been written between 1651 and 1653 for private
performance by the schoolboys Shirley was then teaching. *Cupid and
Death* was revived at the Military Ground in Leicester Fields (on the site
of the present Gerrard Street, Soho) in 1659; and for this revival Locke
made various musical additions to the score, as appears from the
manuscript in the British Library (Add. MS. 17799). In the 19th century
Cupid and Death was transcribed by Edward Jones and part of it scored
by Sir Henry Rowley Bishop (Add. MS. 17800).

1654 ANON: *Cupid his Coronation*
Masque. Text by Thomas Jordan. Four (brief) 'entrances'.[3] 'As it was
Presented with good Approbation at the Spittle diverse tymes by Masters
and yong Ladyes that were theyre Scholers'. See *Fancy's Festivals* (1657).

(1) Bodleian Mus. Sch. B.2.
(2) According to Edward F. Rimbault, the music was by N. Lanier and was printed
at the end of the masque.
(3) Bodleian MS Rawlinson B.165 ff 107–114.

1656 CHARLES COLEMAN, HENRY COOK, H. LAWES, and GEORGE HUDSON: *The First Day's Entertainment*
23 May. Rutland House, Charterhouse Yard
The description of this moral representation is contained in its full title—'*The First Days Entertainment at Rutland-House, by Declamations and Musick: After the Manner of the Ancients*'. Text by W. Davenant. One act. The music has not survived.

H. LAWES, H. COOK, M. LOCKE, C. COLEMAN, and G. HUDSON: *The Siege of Rhodes* [Part I]*
September. Rutland House, Charterhouse Yard
Representation. Text by W. Davenant. Five entries. The description of this representation is contained in its full title—'The Siege of Rhodes Made a Representation by the Art of Prospective in Scenes, and the Story sung in Recitative Musick'. Decorations by John Webb.
It was revived at the Cockpit Theatre in 1658 or 1659, and revised and enlarged for the production at Lincoln's Inn Fields Theatre in June 1661 when it was played with the Second Part. The music has not survived.

1657 ANON: *Fancy's Festivals*
Masque. Text by Thomas Jordan—'as it hath been privately presented by many civil persons of quality'. The Introduction is identical with the Priest's opening speech in *Cupid his Coronation* (1654); and the anti-masque of the nations is also borrowed from Jordan's earlier masque.

1658 VARIOUS COMPOSERS:[1] *The Cruelty of the Spaniards in Peru*
June. Cockpit, Drury Lane
Representation. Text by W. Davenant. Six entries. The description of this representation is contained in its full title—'The Cruelty of the Spaniards in Peru, Exprest by Instrumentall and Vocall Musick, and by Art of Perspective in Scenes, &c.' It was revived at Lincoln's Inn Fields in *The Play-House to be Lett* (summer of 1663). The music has not survived.

1659 M. LOCKE and OTHER COMPOSERS:[1] *The History of Sir Francis Drake**
(?) *May.* Cockpit, Drury Lane
Representation. Text by William Davenant. Six entries. The description of this representation is contained in its full title—'The History of Sir Francis Drake, Exprest by Instrumental and Vocal Musick, and by Art of Perspective in Scenes, &c.' A Symerons' Dance by Locke (probably an extract from the score for this representation) was published in *Musicks Handmaid* about twenty years later. The rest of the music seems to be lost.
Although *The Cruelty of the Spaniards in Peru* and *The History of Sir Francis Drake* were written and produced in that order, they really form the second and first parts respectively of a single work. They were referred to as 'the First and Second Part of Peru' by Sir Henry Herbert, Master of the Revels; and when the quarto of *The History of Sir Francis*

(1) Possibly the same composers as for *The Siege of Rhodes* (1656).

Drake was published in 1659, it bore the subtitle 'The First Part' on the title-page. The two works were played in their correct sequence when they became Acts III and IV of *The Playhouse to be Lett* (1663).

c. 1660   ANON: *The Cheaters Cheated**

Farce jig (called 'a representation in four parts to be sung'). Text by Thomas Jordan. One act.

This lengthy jig of over 500 lines was 'made for the Sheriffs of London' and published in Jordan's *Royal Arbor of Loyal Poesie* (1664). There are directions for eight changes of tune; but none of the nine tunes is specified. The place and date of the first performances are not known.

1661   VARIOUS COMPOSERS:[1] *The Siege of Rhodes* [Part II]**

29(?) June. Lincoln's Inn Fields
Opera.[2] Text by W. Davenant. Five acts.

The entry in the Stationers' Register is dated 30 May 1659. The music has not survived.

1673   M. LOCKE and ROBERT JOHNSON: *Macbeth*

18(?) February. Duke's, Dorset Garden
Dramatic opera.[3] Text by W. Davenant after Shakespeare and Middleton. Five acts.

Most of the Johnson settings are extant, and two of Locke's tunes have been preserved. A new musical setting was made by John Eccles for the 1696 revival. This was not published; but there are several MS copies of the score in the British Library, including Add. MS. 12219, which was used in the theatre. It seems likely that Richard Leveridge wrote the music for a 1702 revival at Drury Lane, which was later published and attributed to Locke.[4]

M. LOCKE: *[Orpheus and Euridice]**

3(?) July. Duke's, Dorset Garden
Masque from Elkanah Settle's *The Empress of Morocco*. Text by Elkanah Settle. One scene.

The manuscript score of this masque, described as '*The groanes of ghosts*: a masque sung by vocall musick, betweene Orpheus, Pluto, Prosserpine, and one woman more, attendantt to Prosserpine' is in Christ Church Library, Oxford (no. 692).

(1) Possibly the same composers as for the first part of *The Siege of Rhodes* (1656).
(2) This term is used by Pepys in his Diary entry for 2 July 1661. 'Went to Sir William Davenant's Opera . . . Today was acted the second part of *The Siege of Rhodes*.'
(3) The term 'dramatic opera' is used here (and elsewhere in this Register) to describe the baroque type of semi-opera popular in England during the last three decades of the 17th century, where the spoken drama is a complete entity in itself and the music is introduced in the form of ancillary entertainments and diversions.
(4) For a full examination of the problems of these different settings, see 'The Music to *Macbeth*' by Robert E. Moore (*The Musical Quarterly*, Vol. XLVII no. 1, January 1961) and 'The *Macbeth* Music' by Roger Fiske (*Music and Letters*, April 1964).

1674 JOHN BANNISTER, GIOVANNI BATTISTA DRAGHI, PELHAM HUMFREY, M. LOCKE, PIETRO REGGIO: *The Tempest*
30(?) April. Duke's, Dorset Garden
Dramatic opera. Text by Thomas Shadwell after the 1667 adaptation of Shakespeare's play by William Davenant and John Dryden. Five acts. Locke's instrumental music was published in 1675.

A subsequent version, with the bulk of the music composed possibly by John Weldon, seems to have been introduced on the London stage about 1710 or 1712. This music was published later in the 18th century, when it was attributed to Henry Purcell.

NATHANIEL STAGGINS: *Calisto, or, The Chaste Nimph*
15 December. Hall Theatre, Whitehall
Masque. Text by John Crowne. Prologue, five acts. The music has not survived.

1675 M. LOCKE and G. B. DRAGHI: *Psyche*
27 February. Duke's Dorset Garden
Dramatic opera. Text by Thomas Shadwell. Five acts.

Locke's music was published under the title 'The English Opera, or, The Vocal Musick in *Psyche* with the Instrumental therein Intermix'd' in 1675.

1676 ANON: *Beauties Triumph*
Chelsea
Masque. Text by Thomas Duffett. One act. 'Presented by the Scholars of Mr Jeffery Banister, and Mr James Hart . . . at Chelsey'.

No music has survived, nor is the name of the composer known, but it is thought it may have been Nathaniel Staggins, or James Hart himself.

1677 JOHN BANNISTER: *Circe*
March. Duke's, Dorset Garden
Dramatic opera. Text by Charles Davenant. Five acts. The music has not survived.

A new musical setting was made by J. E. Galliard in 1719.

1681 JOHN ECCLES: *The Lancashire Witches and Tegue O Divelly the Irish Priest*
c. September. Duke's, Dorset Garden
'A kind of Opera'—W. Downes in Roscius Anglicanus (1708). Text by Thomas Shadwell. The music has not survived.

c. **1682 JOHN BLOW:** *Venus and Adonis**
Whitehall
'A Masque for the Entertainment of the King'. Librettist unknown. Date of first performance likewise unknown. Prologue and three acts.

There are two more or less contemporary manuscripts in the British Library (Add. MS 22100 and Add. MS 31453), one in Christ Church Library, Oxford (no. 37), and one in Westminster Abbey Library (CJ3(1)).

1685   LOUIS GRABU: *Albion and Albanius**
3 June. Queen's, Dorset Garden
Opera. Text by John Dryden. Three acts.
The score was published by subscription in 1687.

1689   HENRY PURCELL: *Dido and Aeneas**
May(?). Mr Priest's School, Chelsea
Opera. Text by Nahum Tate. Three acts and epilogue.
Incorporated as '*The Loves of Dido and Aeneas*, a masque, in four musical entertainments' in Charles Gildon's adaptation of Shakespeare's *Measure for Measure* at Lincoln's Inn Fields in 1700. Revived independently as *The Masque of Aeneas and Dido* at Lincoln's Inn Fields on 29 January and 8 April 1704.
The main source of the music is an 18th century manuscript score, formerly in the possession of the Rev. Sir Frederick Ouseley and now in the Library of St Michael's College, Tenbury Wells (no. 1266). A new realisation was made by Benjamin Britten for the English Opera Group and performed by that company for the first time at the Lyric Theatre, Hammersmith, on 1 May 1951.

1690   H. PURCELL: *The Prophetess, or, The History of Dioclesian*
June. Queen's, Dorset Garden
Dramatic opera. Text by Thomas Betterton, after Fletcher and Massinger. Five acts.
Purcell's score was published by subscription in 1691.

1691   H. PURCELL: *King Arthur, or, The British Worthy*
May. Queen's, Dorset Garden
'A dramatick opera'. Text by John Dryden. Five acts.
A new version entitled *King Arthur, His Magical History* was prepared by Colin Graham and Philip Ledger for the English Opera Group in 1970.

1692   H. PURCELL: *The Fairy Queen*
2 May. Queen's, Dorset Garden
Dramatic opera. Text anon—it is thought the author may have been Elkanah Settle—after Shakespeare's *A Midsummer Night's Dream*. Five acts.
As appears from two advertisements in *The London Gazette* (October 1701), there was a period of time when Purcell's manuscript score was lost: but ultimately it was recovered and is now in the Library of the Royal Academy of Music.

1694   J. ECCLES: *The Rape of Europa by Jupiter**
Dorset Garden
'A masque'. Text attributed to William Ranson. One act. The manuscript of the score is in the British Library (Add. MS. 35043).

1695   H. PURCELL: *Bonduca, or, The British Heroine*
September. Drury Lane
Dramatic opera. Text by George Powell, after Fletcher. Five acts.

H. PURCELL: *The Indian Queen*
Drury Lane
Dramatic opera. Text by John Dryden and Robert Howard (1664).
Prologue, five acts.
  The music for the masque in Act V was written by Daniel Purcell,
Henry's brother. It is possible that the alteration of the text was carried
out by Thomas Betterton.

1696 ### DANIEL PURCELL: *Brutus of Alba, or, Augusta's Triumph*
October. Dorset Garden
Dramatic opera. Text by George Powell and John Verbruggen. Five acts.

GODFREY FINGER and J. ECCLES: *The Loves of Mars and Venus**
12(?) November. Lincoln's Inn Fields
Masque (acted with Edward Ravenscroft's play *The Anatomist*). Text by
Peter Motteux. Prologue, three acts.[1]

D. PURCELL: *Cinthia and Endimion, or, The Loves of the Deities*
December. Drury Lane
'A new opera'. Text by Thomas D'Urfey. Five acts. 'Designed to be acted
at Court before the late Queen.'

1697 ### J. ECCLES: *Hercules**
8 June. Lincoln's Inn Fields
Masque (being the third act of *The Novelty*—'Every Act a Play'). Text by
Peter Motteux. One act.

D. PURCELL and JEREMIAH CLARKE:[2] *The World in the Moon*
29 June. Dorset Garden
'An opera'. Text by Elkanah Settle. Five acts.

ANON: *The Imposture Defeated, or, A Trick to Cheat the Devil*
September. Drury Lane
From the address to the reader:– '. . . this triffle of a Comedy was only a
slight piece of Scribble, purely design'd for the Introduction of a little
Musick, being no more than a short work, to serve the wants of a thin
Playhouse and Long Vacation.' Text by George Powell. Five acts. The
fifth act contains '*Endimion, The Man in the Moon. A masque.*'

(1) The Prologue and Act III were composed by Finger; Acts I and II by Eccles.
With regard to the date of first performance, see the letter written by Robert
Jennens on Thursday 19 November 1696, in which he says 'There has been for four
or five days together at the play house in Lincolns Inn Fields acted a new farce . . .
with a great concert of music, representing the loves of Venus and Mars . . .'
(2) According to the printed libretto, the only numbers composed by Jeremiah
Clarke were the sung Prologue and the entertainment at the end of Act I.

J. ECCLES: *Europe's Revels for the Peace*
29(?) November. Lincoln's Inn Fields
Masque. Text by Peter Motteux. Manuscript full score in the British Library (Add. MS. 29378).

J. ECCLES: *Ixion**
November or December. Lincoln's Inn Fields
Masque. Text by William Taverner. One act. Inserted in Edward Ravenscroft's play *The Italian Husband*.

1698 J. ECCLES: *Rinaldo and Armida*
November. Lincoln's Inn Fields
Dramatic opera. Text by John Dennis, after Tasso. Five acts. The manuscript full score is in the British Library (Add. MS. 29378).

1699 D. PURCELL, J. CLARKE, and RICHARD LEVERIDGE: *The Island Princess, or, The Generous Portuguese*
January. Drury Lane
Dramatic opera. Text by Peter Motteux, after Fletcher. Prologue, five acts. At the end of the last act, a separate entertainment was performed called *The Four Seasons, viz.*

J. CLARKE: *The Four Seasons, or, Love in every Age*
January. Drury Lane
'A Musical Interlude'. Text by Peter Motteux. One act. The manuscript full score of *The Island Princess* is in the British Library (Add. MS. 15318).

1700 D. PURCELL: *The Grove, or, Love's Paradice*
19 February. Drury Lane
Dramatic opera. Text by John Oldmixon. Five acts. The manuscript full score is in the Royal College of Music (988).

D. PURCELL:[1] *The Secular Masque**
25 March. Drury Lane
Masque. Text by John Dryden. One act. Inserted into Sir John Vanbrugh's commedy *The Pilgrim*. The manuscript full score of the first part is in the British Library (Add. MS. 29378).
   A new setting of this masque was made by William Boyce and performed in 1749 (q.v.).

1701 ANON: *Peleus and Thetis**
January.[2] Lincoln's Inn Fields
Masque. Text by George Granville, Lord Lansdowne. One act. Inserted into *The Jew of Venice*, an adaptation of Shakespeare's *The Merchant of Venice*.

---

(1) It is thought that some of the music was by Gottfried Finger. Dryden died just before the first performance; and this was his last work for the stage.
(2) There is no record of the exact date of the first performance of *The Jew of Venice*; but the text was published in January 1701.

A new setting of this masque was made by William Boyce and performed in 1747 (q.v.).

The Judgment of Paris*

On 21 March 1699 an advertisement in *The London Gazette* offered four prizes for settings of William Congreve's one-act masque, *The Judgment of Paris*. In the event 100 guineas were awarded to John Weldon, fifty to John Eccles, thirty to Daniel Purcell, and twenty to Godfrey Finger; and the rival works were performed before the subscribers on the following dates at the Theatre in Dorset Garden:

21 *March* 1701	version by J. Eccles
28 *March* 1701	version by G. Finger
11 *April* 1701	version by D. Purcell
6 *May* 1701	version by J. Weldon
3 *June* 1701	all four versions

The Eccles version was also performed at the Queen's Theatre in the Haymarket on 11 March and 15 April 1706. The Eccles and Purcell scores were published. The manuscript of Weldon's version is in the Folger Shakespeare Library in Washington D.C. Finger's score was lost in the course of his return journey to Vienna.

These different scores must have received a kind of superior concert performance, perhaps in costume. The setting was described in a letter from William Congreve to his Dublin friend, Joseph Keally.

> I don't think any one place in the world can show such an assembly. The number of performers, besides the verse singers, was 85. The front of the stage was all built into a concave with deal boards; all of which was faced with tin, to increase and throw forward the sound . . . The place where formerly the music used to play, between the pit and the stage, was turned into White's chocolate-house; the whole family being transplanted thither with chocolate, cool'd drinks, ratafia, portico, &c., which every body that would call'd for, the whole expense of every thing being defray'd by the subscribers.

A concert setting of Congreve's libretto 'composed for three Quires, and in quite a different way to the others, not used here before' was made by J. W. Franck and performed at York Buildings on 4 February 1702.

G. FINGER: The Virgin Prophetess, or, The Fate of Troy[1]

2 May. Drury Lane
Dramatic opera. Text by Elkanah Settle. Five acts. There are manuscript copies of the full score in the Royal College of Music, London (862), and the Fitzwilliam Museum, Cambridge (23.H.12).

J. ECCLES: Acis and Galatea*

May(?).[2] Drury Lane

---

(1) Later known as *Cassandra, or, The Virgin Prophetess* (1702) and *The Siege of Troy* (1707).
(2) There is no record of the first performance of *Acis and Galatea*, or of *The Mad Lover*; but the text of the songs in *Acis and Galatea* was published in May 1701. By 11 December 1702 it was being performed on its own at Lincoln's Inn Fields.

Masque. Text by Peter Motteux. One act. Inserted in *The Mad Lover*, which may have been an operatic version of Fletcher's play.

D. PURCELL and G. FINGER: *Alexander the Great*
Early summer(?). Drury Lane

The text was based on Nathaniel Lee's *The Rival Queens, or, The Death of Alexander the Great* (1677). The music supplied by Daniel Purcell and Godfrey Finger was incidental; but in John Walsh's publications of Finger's Ayres and Purcell's Songs the work is described as an 'opera'. It is sometimes referred to as *The Rival Queens*. The manuscript full score is in the Fitzwilliam Museum, Cambridge (23.H.12).

1704 J. WELDON and CHARLES DIEUPART: *Britain's Happiness*
22 February. Drury Lane

'A new Entertainment of Vocal and Instrumental Musick, after the manner of an Opera'. Text by Peter Motteux. This was part of Mrs Toft's Subscription Music. Weldon composed the vocal music, and Dieupart the instrumental.

A different setting of the same libretto by Richard Leveridge was performed at the Theatre in Lincoln's Inn Fields about the same time (see Charles Burney, A General History of Music, Vol. IV).

1705 THOMAS CLAYTON, NICOLINO HAYM, and C. DIEUPART: *Arsinoe, Queen of Cyprus**
16 January. Drury Lane

'An opera, after the *Italian* manner: All sung'. Text by Peter Motteux, after Tomaso Stanzani. Three acts. The full score was published, but lacks recitatives and suggests only continuo accompaniment for the arias.

Arsinoe is the first of a series of operas which, strictly speaking, should not qualify for inclusion in a Register aiming primarily at operas written by British composers, for in most cases the bulk of the music was written by Italian composers, the texts were Italian with English translation, and the singers were a mixture of English and Italian. These operas, however, form an important bridge to the introduction of Italian opera in London and the arrival of Handel in 1711. As Handel spent the greater part of the rest of his life in England, becoming naturalised in 1725, his London operatic output, though Italian in style and text, must naturally be included in this Register. The 'mixed' operas leading from *Arsinoe* (1705) to Handel's *Rinaldo* (1711) are

> *The Loves of Ergasto* (1705)
> *The Temple of Love* (1706)
> *Camilla* (1706)
> *Love's Triumph* (1708)
> *Pyrrhus and Demetrius* (1708)
> *Clotilda* (1709)
> *Almahide* (1710)
> *L'Idaspe Fedele* (1710)
> *Etearco* (1710)

JAKOB GREBER: *The Loves of Ergasto**
9 April. Queen's, Haymarket

'A foreign opera, performed by a new set of singers, arrived from Italy' (Downes). Text probably by A. Amalteo (*Gli Amori piacevoli d'Ergasto*, Vienna, 1661). Prologue and three acts.

The indications are that this opera, produced at the inauguration of the Queen's Theatre in the Haymarket, was sung in Italian, and that Greber wrote the music during his residence in London.

1706 **WILLIAM CORBETT:** *The British Enchanters, or, No Magic like Love*
21 February. Queen's, Haymarket
Dramatic opera. Text by George Granville, Lord Lansdowne. Five acts. According to Downes, this 'infinitely arrided both Sexes, and pleas'd the Town as well as any *English* Modern Opera'.

GIUSEPPE SAGGIONE: *The Temple of Love**
7 March. Queen's, Haymarket
Pastoral opera. Text by Peter Motteux ('English'd from the Italian'). Prologue, three acts, and epilogue.

MARCANTONIO BONONCINI: *Camilla**
30 March. Drury Lane
'An opera'. Text by Northman and Motteux. Three acts. Bononcini's score was adapted by Nicolino Haym.

According to the anonymous author of *A Comparison between the French and Italian musick and opera's* (1709), the text was by Silvio Stampiglia and the music by Giovanni Bononcini.

J. ECCLES, JOHN SMITH, G. B. DRAGHI, and J.-B. LULLI: *Wonders in the Sun, or, The Kingdom of the Birds*
5 April. Queen's, Haymarket
Comic opera. Text by Thomas D'Urfey. Prologue and five acts.

1707 **[J. ECCLES:** *Semele**
Opera. Text by William Congreve. Three acts.

This setting of Congreve's *Semele* was possibly intended for the opening of the new Queen's Theatre in the Haymarket in 1705; but Eccles did not finish the score until 1707, by which time public interest had shifted to Italian opera, so the work was not produced. The manuscript full score (for strings alone, with a few passages omitted) is in the Royal College of Music, London.

In 1964 a musical arrangement of Eccles's music was made by Stoddart Lincoln;[1] and this version was first performed on 4 June 1964 in the Holywell Music Room, Oxford.]

T. CLAYTON: *Rosamond**
4 March. Drury Lane
Opera. Text by Joseph Addison. Three acts. The full score was published, but lacks recitatives and suggests only continuo accompaniments for the arias.

(1) See 'Eccles and Congreve: Music and Drama on the Restoration stage' by Stoddart Lincoln. *Theatre Notebook*, XVIII, 1, 1963.

A new setting with music by T. A. Arne was produced at the Theatre in Lincoln's Inn Fields in 1733 (q.v.).

JOHN CHRISTOPHER PEPUSCH and OTHERS: *Thomyris, Queen of Scythia**
1 April. Drury Lane
Opera. Text by Peter Motteux. Three acts.

 A pasticcio opera to music by A. Scarlatti and G. Bononcini—also Steffani, Gasparini, and Albinoni—arranged by Pepusch, who provided the recitative.

1708 **ANON:** *The Coy Shepherdess*
Dublin
'A pastoral'. Text by Tony Aston.

 It appears that a later version, entitled *Pastora, or, The Coy Shepherdess* and described as an opera, was performed by the Duke of Richmond's Servants at Tunbridge Wells in 1712, presumably in the Assembly Rooms on the Walks (Pantiles).

VARIOUS COMPOSERS: *Prunella**
12 February. Drury Lane
Interlude. Text by Richard Estcourt. Performed (apparently between the acts) during a revival of *The Rehearsal* by George Villiers, Duke of Buckingham.

CARLO CESARINI, GIOVANNINO DEL VIOLONE, and FRANCISCO GASPARINI: *Love's Triumph**
26 February. Queen's, Haymarket
Opera. English text by Peter Motteux, after Ottoboni's *La Pastorella*. Three acts.

 According to Motteux, Dieupart helped 'in the Contrivance of the Entertainments' and supplied 'what Recitative and other Music was necessary'. It was given in English, with the exception of the part of Liso, which was sung by Valentino in Italian. Each of the three Italian composers seems to have been responsible for the music of one of the three acts.

A. SCARLATTI and N. HAYM: *Pyrrhus and Demetrius**
14 December. Queen's, Haymarket
Opera. Italian text by A. Morselli for the original opera by Scarlatti (1694) translated partly by Owen Swiney and Armstrong. The Scarlatti score was edited by Haym, who added twenty-one airs of his own. Three acts. Sung partly in English and partly in Italian.

1709 **F. CONTINI, A. SCARLATTI, and G. BONONCINI:** *Clotilda**
2 March. Queen's, Haymarket
Pasticcio. Original Italian text by G. B. Neri. Sung partly in English and partly in Italian.

1710 **G. BONONCINI(?):** *Almahide**
10 January. Queen's, Haymarket

Opera. Librettist unknown. Three acts. Sung partly in Italian and partly in English.

FRANCESCO MANCINI: *L'Idaspe Fedele (Hydaspes)**
23 March. Queen's, Haymarket
Opera. Italian text by G. A. Cicognini.
   The cast was completely Italian, with the exception of Mr Lawrence, who, however, sang his part in Italian. The first performance was preceded by a 'Practice of the new Opera in Form' (*The Daily Courant*) at the Queen's Theatre on 6 March.

G. BONONCINI: *Etearco**
20 December. Queen's, Haymarket
Opera. Italian text by Silvio Stampiglia.
   From this point onwards the only 'Italian' operas included in this Register are those composed by G. F. Handel.

1711 GEORGE FREDERIC HANDEL: *Rinaldo**
24 February. Queen's, Haymarket
Opera. Italian text by Lauro Rossi after Tasso: English translation by Aaron Hill. Three acts. Sung in Italian. Handel's first opera for London.

1712 JOHN ERNEST GALLIARD: *Calypso and Telemachus*
14 May. Queen's, Haymarket
Dramatic opera opera. Text by John Hughes. Three acts. The full score was published.

G. F. HANDEL: *Il Pastor Fido**
22 November. Queen's, Haymarket
Opera. Italian text by Lauro Rossi, after G. B. Guarini. Three acts.

1713 G. F. HANDEL: *Teseo**
10 January. Queen's, Haymarket
Opera. Italian text by Nicolino Haym, adapted from Philippe Quinault. Five acts.

G. F. HANDEL: *Silla**
2 June. Burlington House
Opera. The only known copy of the Italian libretto is in the Huntington Library, San Marino, California. Privately performed.

1715 J. C. PEPUSCH: *Venus and Adonis**
12 March. Drury Lane
Masque. Text by Colley Cibber 'in English, but after the Italian manner'. Two interludes. The manuscript full score is in the Royal College of Music, London.

G. F. HANDEL: *Amadigi di Gaula**
25 May. King's, Haymarket
Opera. Italian text probably by J. J. Heidegger, adapted from Houdar de la Motte. Three acts.

J. C. PEPUSCH: *Myrtillo*
5 November. Drury Lane
'Pastoral masque'. Text by Colley Cibber. 'Composed after the Italian manner.'

1716   ### J. C. PEPUSCH: *Apollo and Daphne*
12 January. Drury Lane
Masque. Text by J. Hughes. One act.

W. TURNER: *Presumptuous Love*
10 March. Lincoln's Inn Fields
Dramatic masque. Text by William Taverner. Two acts. This masque was introduced into Taverner's comedy, *Every Body Mistaken*.

R. LEVERIDGE: *The Comick Masque of Pyramus and Thisbe*
11 April. Lincoln's Inn Fields
Masque. Text by the composer. One act.
See also *Pyramus and Thisbe* (1745).

J. C. PEPUSCH: *The Death of Dido*
17 April. Drury Lane
Masque. Text by Barton Booth. One act.

1718   ### J. E. GALLIARD: *Pan and Syrinx**
14 January. Lincoln's Inn Fields
Opera. Text by Lewis Theobald. One act. The autograph manuscript full score is in the British Library (Add. MS. 31588) and includes all the recitatives.

ANON: *Amadis, or, The Loves of Harlequin and Columbine*
24 January. Lincoln's Inn Fields
'Dramatick opera'. Author of text unknown. One act.
   One of John Rich's elaborate pantomimes.[1]

J. E. GALLIARD: *The Lady's Triumph*
22 March. Lincoln's Inn Fields
Comic-dramatic opera. Text of the play by Elkanah Settle; text of the 'entertainments set to music' by Lewis Theobald. Five acts.
   These entertainments included the masque of *Decius and Paulina*, which was also used in *Circe* (11 April 1719).

1720   ### G. F. HANDEL: *Il Radamisto**
27 April. King's, Haymarket
Opera. Italian text by N. F. Haym. Three acts. The first opera written by Handel for the Royal Academy of Music.

1721   ### F. MATTEI, G. BONONCINI, G. F. HANDEL: *Il Muzio Scevola**

(1) For a good definition of 'pantomime' during this period see Nicoll.

15 April. King's, Haymarket
Opera. Italian text by P. A. Rolli. Three acts, the first being composed by
Mattei, the second by Bononcini, and the third by Handel.

G. F. HANDEL: *Il Floridante**
9 December. King's, Haymarket
Opera. Italian text by P. A. Rolli. Three acts.

1722 ### ANON: *Love Triumphant, or, The Rival Goddesses*
Easter Monday. Mrs Bellamy's School
Pastoral opera. Text by Daniel Bellamy, senior and junior.

1723 ### G. F. HANDEL: *Ottone, Re di Germania**
12 January. King's, Haymarket
Opera. Italian text by N. F. Haym. Three acts.

COBSTON, J. E. GALLIARD, R. LEVERIDGE: *Jupiter and Europa, or, The Intrigues of Harlequin*
23 March. Lincoln's Inn Fields
'Masque of songs'. One of John Rich's elaborate pantomimes. Text by R.
Leveridge.

G. F. HANDEL: *Flavio, Re de' Longobardi**
14 May. King's, Haymarket
Opera. Italian text by N. F. Haym, after Corneille. Three acts.

ANON: *The Necromancer, or, Harlequin Doctor Faustus*
20 December. Lincoln's Inn Fields
'Masque of songs'. One of John Rich's elaborate pantomimes. Author of
text unknown.

1724 ### G. F. HANDEL: *Giulio Cesare in Egitto**
20 February. King's, Haymarket
Opera. Italian text by N. F. Haym. Three acts.

G. F. HANDEL: *Tamerlano**
31 October. King's, Haymarket
Opera. Italian text by A. Salvi, adapted by N. F. Haym. Three acts.

1725 ### G. F. HANDEL: *Rodelinda**
13 February. King's, Haymarket
Opera. Italian text by A. Salvi, adapted by N. F. Haym. Three acts.

ANON: *Harlequin, a Sorcerer, With the Loves of Pluto and Proserpine*
21 February. Lincoln's Inn Fields
One of John Rich's elaborate pantomimes. Text by Lewis Theobald. One
act.

1726 J. E. GALLIARD: *Apollo and Daphne, or, The Burgo-Master trick'd*
15 January. Lincoln's Inn Fields
One of John Rich's elaborate pantomimes. Text by Lewis Theobald. One act.

G. F. HANDEL: *Scipione**
12 March. King's, Haymarket
Opera. Italian text by P. A. Rolli. Three acts.

1727 G. F. HANDEL: *Admeto,*[1] *Re di Tessaglia**
31 January. King's, Haymarket
Opera. Italian text based on an earlier libretto by Aurelio Aureli. Three acts.

J. E. GALLIARD: *The Rape of Proserpine*
14 February. Lincoln's Inn Fields
One of John Rich's elaborate pantomimes. Text by Lewis Theobald. One act. An overture and fourteen songs by Galliard were published in full score.

ANON: *Great Britain Rejoycing**
22 October (n.s.). Hamburg, Opera-house
'Musical entertainment'. Text by Thomas Lediard. Three acts.
    This was specially composed to celebrate the coronation of George II and was given two performances in the Hamburg opera-house in the Goosemarket—one for ministers and local worthies, and the other for the English residents.

G. F. HANDEL: *Riccardo primo, Re d'Inghilterra**
11 November. King's, Haymarket
Opera. Italian text by P. A. Rolli. Three acts.

1728 ANON: *The Beggar's Opera*
29 January. Lincoln's Inn Fields
Ballad opera. Music arranged by J. C. Pepusch. Text by John Gay. Three acts. The ballad airs were published with the libretto.
    There have been numerous revivals of this, the first and most popular of all the ballad operas. The following musical adaptations deserve special mention:– On 5 June 1920 it was produced by Nigel Playfair at the Lyric Theatre, Hammersmith, with designs by Lovat Fraser and in a musical version by Frederic Austin and ran for 1,463 performances. An edition prepared by Edward J. Dent was first performed in the Big Top, Birmingham, on 22 May 1944. Benjamin Britten made a new realisation for the English Opera Group, which received its first performance at the Arts Theatre, Cambridge, on 24 March 1948.

G. F. HANDEL: *Siroe, Re di Persia**
17 February. King's, Haymarket
Opera. Italian text by P. Metastasio, adapted by N. F. Haym. Three acts.

(1) Sometimes referred to in the 18th century as *Ammeto*.

ANON: *The Cobler's Opera*
26 April. Lincoln's Inn Fields
Ballad opera. Text by Lacy Ryan. The ballad airs were published with the libretto.

G. F. HANDEL: *Tolomeo, Re di Egitto**
30 April. King's, Haymarket
Opera. Italian text by N. F. Haym. Three acts.

ANON: *Penelope*
8 May. Little Theatre, Haymarket
Ballad opera. Text by John Mottley and Thomas Cooke. Three acts. The ballad airs were published with the libretto.

ANON: *The Quaker's Opera*
24 September. Bartholomew Fair
Ballad opera. Text by Thomas Walker. Three acts.
   The production moved from 'Lee's and Harper's great theatrical booth in Bartholomew Fair' to the Little Theatre in the Haymarket on 31 October 1728. The ballad airs were published with the libretto.

ANON: *The Craftsman, or, Weekly Journalist*
15 October. Little Theatre, Haymarket
Ballad opera. Text by John Mottley.

[ANON: *Polly*
Ballad opera. Music arranged by J. C. Pepusch. Text by John Gay. Three acts.
   This sequel to *The Beggar's Opera* was ready for production towards the end of 1728; but on 12 December Gay heard from the Lord Chamberlain 'that it was not allow'd to be acted, but commanded to be supprest'.
   The first performance was given at the Theatre Royal, Haymarket, on 19 June 1777, when Samuel Arnold provided extra musical numbers. On 30 December 1922 it was produced by Nigel Playfair at the Lyric Theatre, Hammersmith, in a version with the music arranged by Frederic Austin and the text by Clifford Bax.
   The ballad airs were published with the libretto in 1729.]

1729   ANON: *Love in a Riddle*
7 January. Drury Lane
Ballad opera. Text by Colley Cibber. Three acts. The ballad airs were published with the libretto.
   See also *Damon and Phillida* (1729) and *Damon and Phillida* (1768).

ANON: *The Gentle Shepherd*
29 January. Edinburgh, Taylor's Hall
'Scots pastoral comedy'. Text by Allan Ramsay. Five acts.
   First published as a pastoral comedy in 1725 with only four songs: changed into a ballad opera with twenty songs in 1729. (See also *Patie and Peggy*, 1730.) The ballad airs were published in a later edition of the libretto.

ANON: *The Village Opera*
6 February. Drury Lane
Ballad opera. Text by Charles Johnson. Three acts. The ballad airs were published with the libretto.

For the altered version made in 1762, see *Love in a Village* (1762).

A new arrangement of the original ballad opera was made in 1929 by Michael Tippett for performance at the Barn Theatre, Oxted.

ANON: *The Beggar's Wedding*
24 March. Dublin, Smock Alley
Ballad opera. Text by Charles Coffey. Three acts. The ballad airs were published with the libretto.

A one-act version entitled *Phebe* was performed at Drury Lane on 13 June 1729.

ANON: *The Devil upon Two Sticks, or, The Country Beau*
16 April. Drury Lane
Ballad opera. Text by Charles Coffey.

ANON: *Flora, an Opera made from Hob, or, The Country Wake*
18 April. Lincoln's Inn Fields
Ballad opera. Text by J. Hippisley. Two acts. The ballad airs were published with the libretto.

ANON: *The Wedding*
6 May. Lincoln's Inn Fields
'A tragi-comi-pastoral-farcical opera.' Text by Essex Hawker. One act.

The overture was composed by Dr Pepusch. The ballad airs were published with the libretto.

ANON: *The Patron, or, The Statesman's Opera*
7 May. Little Theatre, Haymarket
Ballad opera. Text by Thomas Odell. Two acts. The ballad airs were published with the libretto.

ANON: *The Lover's Opera*
14 May. Drury Lane
Ballad opera. Text by W. R. Chetwood. One act. The ballad airs were published with the libretto.

HENRY CAREY: *The Contrivances*
20 June. Drury Lane
'Ballad opera'. Text by the composer. One act.

The Contrivances was originally produced as a farce (Drury Lane, 9 August 1715). In Carey's dramatic works (published in 1743) this alteration was styled 'a ballad opera'; but a note was added saying 'All the Songs in this *Opera* were set to Music by the Author'.

ANON: *Damon and Phillida*
16 August. Little Theatre, Haymarket

Ballad opera. Text by Colley Cibber. One act. Based on material from *Love in a Riddle* (1729).

G. F. HANDEL: *Lotario**
2 December. King's, Haymarket
Opera. Italian text by A. Salvi. Three acts.

ANON: *Momus turn'd Fabulist, or, Vulcan's Wedding*
3 December. Lincoln's Inn Fields
Ballad opera. Text by Ebenezer Forrest, after L. Fuzelier. Three acts. The ballad airs were published with the libretto.

1730 ## ANON: *Perseus and Andromeda*
2 January. Lincoln's Inn Fields
One of John Rich's elaborate pantomimes. Text by Lewis Theobald.

ANON: *The Chambermaid*
10 February. Drury Lane
Ballad opera. Text by Edward Phillips. One act.

G. F. HANDEL: *Partenope**
20 February. King's, Haymarket
Opera. Italian text by Silvio Stampiglia. Three acts.

ANON: *Bayes's Opera*
30 March. Drury Lane
Ballad opera. Text by Gabriel Odingsells. Three acts.

ANON: *The Author's Farce, and The Pleasures of the Town*
30 March. Little Theatre, Haymarket
Ballad opera. Text by Henry Fielding. Three acts.

ANON: *The Fashionable Lady, or, Harlequin's Opera*
2 April. Goodman's Fields
Burlesque 'in the manner of a rehearsal'. Text by James Ralph. One act. The ballad airs were published with the libretto.

ANON: *The Female Parson, or, Beau in the Sudds*
27 April. Little Theatre, Haymarket
Ballad opera. Text by Charles Coffey. Three acts. The ballad airs were published with the libretto.

ANON: *The Prisoner's Opera**
Summer. Sadler's Wells
Ballad opera. Text attributed to Edward Ward. One act.
As speaking on the stage was illegal at Sadler's Wells, there is no spoken dialogue. The ballad airs were published with the libretto.[1]

(1) A copy of this rare libretto is to be found in the British Library, bound up with the first of three MS notebooks on 18th century drama made by Francis Place (Add. MS. 27831).

H. CAREY, RICHARD CHARKE, JOHN SHEELES:
The Generous Free-Mason, or, The Constant Lady
20 August. Bartholomew Fair
'A tragi-comi-farcical ballad opera.' Text by W. R. Chetwood. Three acts. Subsequently produced at the Little Theatre in the Haymarket on 28 December 1730. The ballad airs were published with the libretto.

ANON: *Robin Hood*
22 August. Bartholomew Fair
Ballad opera. Three acts. The ballad airs were published with the libretto.

H. CAREY: *Cephalus and Procris*
28 October. Drury Lane
Dramatic masque. One act.

ANON: *Silvia, or, The Country Burial*
10 November. Lincoln's Inn Fields
'An opera'. Text by George Lillo. Three acts. The ballad airs were published with the libretto.

ANON: *Patie and Peggy, or, The Fair Foundling*
25 November.[1] Drury Lane
'A Scotch ballad opera'. Text by Theophilus Cibber. One act. (A reduction of *The Gentle Shepherd*, 1729.)

ANON: *The Jealous Clown, or, The Lucky Mistake*
16 December. Goodman's Fields
Ballad opera. Text by Thomas Gataker. One act. The ballad airs were published with the libretto.

1731 ANON: *The Fool's Opera, or, The Taste of the Age*
? Oxford
Ballad opera. Text by Tony Aston ('written by Mat. Medley and performed by his company in Oxford'). The date of the first performance is not known: but the libretto was published on 1 April 1731.[2]

ANON: *The Jealous Taylor, or, The Intriguing Valet*
14 January. Little Theatre, Haymarket
Ballad opera.

G. F. HANDEL: *Poro, Re dell'Indie**
2 February. King's, Haymarket
Opera. Metastasio's Italian libretto for *Alessandro* under a new title. Three acts.

ANON: *The Jovial Crew*
8 February. Drury Lane

(1) It is to be noted that Theophilus Cibber's preface to the libretto is dated 20 April 1730: so the piece may have been produced before November.
(2) See R. H. Griffith, 'Tony Aston's "Fool's Opera"', *Journal of English and Germanic Philology*, 1922, xxi.

Ballad opera. Text by E. Roome, M. Concanen, and Sir William Yonge after the play by R. Brome. Three acts. The ballad airs were published with the libretto.

A revised version was brought out at Covent Garden on 14 February 1760 with the score revised by William Bates. (See also *The Ladies' Frolick*, 1770.)

ANON: *The Highland Fair, or, Union of the Clans*
20 March. Drury Lane
Ballad opera. The music consisted of 'Select Scots Tunes'. Text by Joseph Mitchell. Three acts. The ballad airs were published with the libretto.

ANON: *Orestes*
3 April. Lincoln's Inn Fields
Dramatic opera. Text by Lewis Theobald. Five acts.

ANON: *The Welsh Opera, or, The Grey Mare the Better Horse*
22 April. Little Theatre, Haymarket
Ballad opera. Text by Henry Fielding.

Later in the season it appears to have been revised and lengthened under the title *The Grub-Street Opera*.

ANON: *The Judgment of Paris*
4 May. Lincoln's Inn Fields
Pastoral ballad opera. Author of the text unknown. One act.

ANON: *The Devil to Pay, or, The Wives Metamorphos'd*
6 August. Drury Lane
Ballad opera. Text by Charles Coffey and John Mottley. Three acts (later reduced to one). The ballad airs were published with the libretto.

This proved to be one of the most successful ballad operas, and for many years it was played regularly at the patent houses. Later operas based on the same text are *The Devil's In It* (1852) and *Letty the Basket-Maker* (1871).

1732 ### ANON: *The Lottery*
1 January. Drury Lane
Ballad opera. Text by Henry Fielding. One act. The ballad airs were published with the libretto.

G. F. HANDEL: *Ezio**
15 January. King's, Haymarket
Opera. Italian text by Metastasio. Three acts.

G. F. HANDEL: *Sosarme, Re di Media**
15 February. King's, Haymarket
Opera. Italian text by Matteo Noris. Three acts.

J. F. LAMPE: *Amelia**
13 March. Little Theatre, Haymarket
'A new English opera after the Italian manner'. Text by Henry Carey. Three acts.

ANON: *A Sequel to the Opera of Flora*
20 March. Lincoln's Inn Fields
Ballad opera. Text by John Hippisley. One act. The ballad airs were published with the libretto.

G. F. HANDEL: *Acis and Galatea**
17 May. Little Theatre, Haymarket
'An English Pastoral Opera.' Text by John Gay. Three acts.

There were earlier non-theatrical productions of *Acis and Galatea*, including its presumed first performance as a 'masque' before the Duke of Chandos at Cannons about 1720, and its performance as a 'pastoral' at Lincoln's Inn Fields on 26 March 1731. Its production as a 'pastoral opera' at the Little Theatre in the Haymarket (17 May 1732) under Thomas Arne, the father of Dr T. A. Arne the composer, was advertised as 'the first time it was ever performed in a theatrical way'. It was followed by a series of performances as a 'serenata' without stage action, but with scenery, given under Handel's direct supervision at the King's Theatre in the Haymarket starting on 10 June 1732.

ANON: *The Mock Doctor, or, The Dumb Lady Cur'd*
23 June. Drury Lane
Ballad opera. Text by Henry Fielding, after Molière. One act. The ballad airs were published with the libretto.

ANON: *The Devil of a Duke, or, Trapolin's Vagaries*
17 August. Drury Lane
'A (farcical ballad) opera'. Text by Robert Drury. One act. The ballad airs were published with the libretto.

J. F. LAMPE: *Britannia**
16 November. Little Theatre, Haymarket
'An English Opera'. Text by Thomas Lediard. 'The Musick compos'd after the Italian manner.'

J. C. SMITH: *Teraminta**
20 November. Lincoln's Inn Fields
Opera. Text by Henry Carey. Three acts. The manuscript full score is in the Royal College of Music (1020).

It has been suggested that the music of *Teraminta* may be by John Stanley, not J. C. Smith. For a full discussion of this theory see Roger Fiske: *English Theatre Music in the Eighteenth Century* (London, 1973) and Mollie Sands: "The Problem of Teraminta", *Music and Letters*, July 1952.

ANON: *Betty, or, The Country Bumpkins*
1 December. Drury Lane
Ballad opera. Text by H. Carey.

1733 ### G. F. HANDEL: *Orlando**
27 January.[1] King's, Haymarket Opera. Italian text by G. Bracciuoli. Three acts.

(1) The date for the first production of *Orlando* is usually given as 23 January; but (according to William C. Smith's *Concerning Handel*) this is incorrect.

ANON: *The Boarding-School, or, The Sham Captain*
29 January. Drury Lane
Ballad opera. Text by Charles Coffey. One act. The ballad airs were published with the libretto.

ANON: *The Decoy, or, The Harlot's Progress*
5 February. Goodman's Fields
Ballad opera. Text by Henry Potter. Three acts. The ballad airs were published with the libretto.

ANON: *Achilles*
10 February. Covent Garden
Ballad opera. Text by John Gay. Three acts. The ballad airs were published with the libretto.

J. F. LAMPE: *Dione*
23 February. Little Theatre, Haymarket
Opera. Author of the text unknown.

ANON: *The Mad Captain*
5 March. Goodman's Fields
Ballad opera. Text by Robert Drury. One act.

T. A. ARNE: *Rosamond**
7 March. Lincoln's Inn Fields
Opera. Text by Joseph Addison. Three acts. (For the original setting by T. Clayton, see under the year 1707.)

ANON: *The Harlot's Progress, or, The Ridotto al Fresco*
31 March. Drury Lane
'A grotesque pantomime entertainment'. Text by Theophilus Cibber.

J. C. SMITH: *Ulysses**
16 April. Lincoln's Inn Fields
Opera. Text by Samuel Humphreys.
   The manuscript full score is in the Hamburg Staats-und-Universitätsbibliothek (MA/279).

ANON: *The Mock Lawyer*
27 April. Covent Garden
Ballad opera. Text by Edward Phillips. One act.

ANON: *The Livery Rake and Country Lass*
5 May. Drury Lane
Ballad opera. Text by Edward Phillips. One act. The ballad airs were published with the libretto.

T. A. ARNE: *The Opera of Operas, or, Tom Thumb the Great*
31 May. Little Theatre, Haymarket
Text by Mrs Eliza Haywood and William Hatchett, after the burlesque by Henry Fielding, 'set to Musick after the Italian Manner'. Three acts. Later, revived in a one-act version.

An altered version of this opera, with music by J. F. Lampe, was brought out at Drury Lane on 7 November 1733.

ANON: *The Fancy'd Queen*
14 August. Covent Garden
Ballad opera. Text by Robert Drury.

ANON: *Timon in Love, or, The Innocent Theft*
5 December. Drury Lane
Ballad opera. Text by John Kelly, after Delisle.

ANON: *The Downfall of Bribery, or, The Honest Men of Taunton*
Taunton
According to the printed text, this was 'A New Ballad Opera of Three Acts. As it was lately perform'd by a Company of Players at a certain noted Inn at Taunton in Somersetshire. By Mark Freeman, of the said Town, Freeholder, and Grocer.' The titlepage carries the following quotation from *The Craftsman* no. 385, 24 November 1733:– 'A few persons at Taunton, who had it in their power to turn the election of a mayor, lately refused a sum of two thousand pounds for their votes upon that occasion.'

ANON: *The Oxford Act*
Oxford
Ballad opera. 'Perform'd by a Company of Students at Oxford'. In the libretto there is a reference to Handel's attendance at the Public Act at Oxford in the summer of 1733—'that cursed Handel, with his confounded Oratorio's'.

1734   T. A. ARNE: *Dido and Aeneas*
12 January. Little Theatre, Haymarket
Masque with harlequinade.

ANON: *The Intriguing Chambermaid*
15 January. Drury Lane
Ballad farce. Text by Henry Fielding from a French farce by Regnard. One act. The ballad airs were published with the libretto.

G. F. HANDEL: *Ariadne in Crete**
26 January. King's, Haymarket
Opera. Italian text by Francis Colman, possibly after Pietro Pariati. Three acts.

J. F. LAMPE: *Cupid and Psyche, or, Colombine-Courtezan*
4 February. Drury Lane
'A dramatic pantomime entertainment'. Author unknown. One act.

ANON: *Don Quixote in England*
5 April. Little Theatre, Haymarket
Text by Henry Fielding. Three acts. The ballad airs were published with the libretto.

ANON: *The Whim, or, The Miser's Retreat*
Goodman's Fields
Ballad opera. Altered from the French of *La maison rustique*. One act. The ballad airs were published with the libretto in 1734.

MAURICE GREENE: *Florimel, or, Love's Revenge**
Winchester, Farnham Castle
'A dramatic pastoral'. Text by John Hoadly. Two acts. Manuscripts of the full score are in the British Library, King's Music Library (22.d.14), and Add. MS. 5324, and also in the Royal College of Music (226). The first performance was in the house of Hoadly's father, the Bishop of Winchester. There was also a performance at the Three Choirs Festival, Gloucester, in 1745.

1735 ### ANON: *An Old Man Taught Wisdom, or, The Virgin Unmask'd*
6 January. Drury Lane
Ballad opera. Text by Henry Fielding. One act. The ballad airs were published with the libretto.

G. F. HANDEL: *Ariodante**
8 January. Covent Garden
Opera. Italian text by Antonio Salvi. Three acts.

ANON: *The Plot*
22 January. Drury Lane
Ballad opera. Text by John Kelly. One act. The ballad airs were published with the libretto.

ANON: *A Cure for a Scold*
25 February. Drury Lane
Ballad farce. Text by James Worsdale, after Shakespeare's *The Taming of the Shrew*. Two acts.

G. F. HANDEL: *Alcina**
16 April. Covent Garden
Opera. Italian text by Antonio Marchi. Three acts.

ANON: *The Merry Cobler, or, The Second Part of The Devil to Pay*
6 May. Drury Lane
Ballad opera. Text by Charles Coffey. One act. (See *The Devil to Pay*, 1731.) The ballad airs were published with the libretto.

ANON: *Trick for Trick*
10 May. Drury Lane
Ballad opera. Text by R. Fabian. Two acts. The Ballad airs were published with the libretto.

ANON: *The Honest Yorkshireman*
15 July. Little Theatre, Haymarket

Ballad opera. Text by Henry Carey. One act. The airs, which Carey
composed or arranged, were published with the libretto.

1736   ANON: *The Rival Milliners, or, The Humours of*
          Covent-Garden
          19 January. Little Theatre, Haymarket
          'A Tragi-Comi-Operatic-Pastoral Farce.' Text by Robert Drury.

          ANON: *The Lover his own Rival*
          10 February. Goodman's Fields
          Ballad opera. Text by Abraham Langford. One act. The ballad airs were
          published with the libretto.

          ANON: *The Female Rake, or, Modern Fine Lady*
          26 April. Little Theatre, Haymarket
          Ballad opera. Text by Joseph Dorman.

          G. F. HANDEL: *Atalanta**
          12 May. Covent Garden
          Opera. Author of the Italian text unknown. Three acts.

          ANON: *The Rival Captains, or, The Imposter Unmasked*
          26 May. Little Theatre, Haymarket
          Ballad opera. Text by Thomas Phillips.

1737   G. F. HANDEL: *Arminio**
          12 January. Covent Garden
          Opera. Italian text by Antonio Salvi. Three acts.

          G. F. HANDEL: *Giustino**
          16 February. Covent Garden
          Opera. Italian text by N. Beregani. Three acts.

          J. F. LAMPE: *The Dragon of Wantley**
          10 May. Little Theatre, Haymarket
          Burlesque opera. Text by Henry Carey. Three acts. The date given is that
          of the first public rehearsal. The official first performance was on 16 May.
          The opera was transferred to Covent Garden on 26 October 1737. The
          full score was published.

          G. F. HANDEL: *Berenice**
          18 May. Covent Garden
          Opera. Italian text by Antonio Salvi. Three acts.

          ANON: *Macheath turn'd Pyrate, or, Polly in India*
          30 May. Little Theatre, Haymarket
          Ballad opera.

1738   G. F. HANDEL: *Faramondo**
          3 January. King's, Haymarket
          Opera. Italian text by A. Zeno. Three acts.

HENRY BURGESS jun. and H. CAREY: *The Coffee House*
26 January. Drury Lane
'A dramatick piece'. Text by the Rev. James Miller. One act.

G. F. HANDEL: *Alessandro Severo**
25 February. King's, Haymarket
Pasticcio. Italian text by A. Zeno(?). Three acts.

T. A. ARNE: *Comus*
4 March. Drury Lane
Masque. Text adapted by Dr John Dalton from Milton's *Comus* (1634). Three acts. The manuscript full score is in the British Library (Add. MS. 11518).

G. F. HANDEL: *Serse**
15 April. King's, Haymarket
Comic opera. Italian text by N. Minato, after Silvio Stampiglia. Three acts.

ANON: *The Lucky Discovery, or, The Tanner of York*
24 April. Covent Garden
'An opera'. Text by John Arthur.

J. F. LAMPE: *Margery, or, A Worse Plague than the Dragon**
9 December. Covent Garden
Burlesque opera. Text by H. Carey. Three acts. A sequel to *The Dragon of Wantley* (1737). The full score was published.

1739 **H. CAREY:** *Nancy, or, The Parting Lovers**
1 December. Covent Garden
Interlude. Text by the composer. One act.
   This was later altered as *The Press Gang, or, Love in Low Life* (1755), since when it has been frequently revived under the title of *True Blue*.

ANON: *Britons, Strike Home! or, The Sailor's Rehearsal*
31 December. Drury Lane
'Farce' or ballad opera. Text by Edward Phillips. One act.

1740 **J. C. SMITH:** *Rosalinda**
4 January. London, Hickford's Room
Musical drama. Text by John Lockman. One act. The libretto contains an interesting preface entitled 'An Enquiry into the Rise and Progress of Operas and Oratorios'.

J. F. LAMPE: *Orpheus and Eurydice*
12 February. Covent Garden
'Dramatic entertainment of music'. Text by Lewis Theobald.
   Towards the end of January 1740 it appears that the 'harlequinade' part of a one-act pantomime entertainment entitled *Orpheus and Eurydice*, written by Henry Sommer and with music also by Lampe, was performed at Lincoln's Inn Fields Theatre.

PETER PRELLEUR: *Baucis and Philemon, or, The Wandering Deities*
7 April. London, New Wells[1]
This opera contained 'a New Pantomime called Harlequin Mountebank'.

T. A. ARNE: *Alfred*
1 August. Clifden, Buckinghamshire
Masque. Text by James Thomson. Two acts.
Performed in a revised version as an opera (all sung) at Drury Lane on 20 March 1745. Later, Charles Burney set a version of the libretto, which had been altered by David Mallet, and this was performed at Drury Lane on 23 February 1751. Subsequently, Arne carried out further revisions, and a full score was published (probably in 1753).[2]

G. F. HANDEL: *Imeneo**
22 November. Lincoln's Inn Fields
Opera. Author of the Italian text unknown.

1741 **G. F. HANDEL:** *Deidamia**
10 January. Lincoln's Inn Fields
Opera. Italian text by Paolo Rolli. Three acts. The last opera Handel composed for London.

T. A. ARNE: *The Blind Beggar of Bethnal Green*
3 April. Drury Lane
Ballad opera. Text by Robert Dodsley. One act.

J. E. GALLIARD: *The Happy Captive . . . with an Interlude, in Two Comick Scenes, Betwixt Signor Capoccio, a Director from the Canary Islands, and Signora Dorinna, A Virtuosa*
16 April. Little Theatre, Haymarket
Interlude. Text by Lewis Theobald. Subsequently, the text of this interlude was incorporated in *The Temple of Dullness* (1745).

J. F. LAMPE: *The Queen of Spain, or, Farinelli in Madrid*
16 April. Dublin, Aungier Street
Musical entertainment. Text by James Worsdale.

1742 **T. A. ARNE:** *The Judgment of Paris*
12 March. Drury Lane
Masque. Text by W. Congreve. One act. (See also under 1701.) The full score was published.
It is sometimes suggested that this masque was first performed on 1 August 1740 at Clifden, Buckinghamshire; but this is erroneous. The version of *The Judgment of Paris* performed on that occasion had music by Giuseppe Sammartini.

---

(1) The New Wells Theatre was close to the Goodman's Fields Theatre.
(2) For a full and detailed account of all the versions of *Alfred*, see Roger Fiske, *English Theatre Music in the Eighteenth Century*. O.U.P. 1973.

ANON: *Miss Lucy in Town*
6 May. Drury Lane
'A farce with songs'. Text by H. Fielding. Written as a sequel to *An Old Man Taught Wisdom* (1735).

1744 G. F. HANDEL: *Semele**
10 February. Covent Garden
Presented as an oratorio: but the English text by William Congreve is the same as that for the opera libretto (1707) he wrote for John Eccles.

J. F. LAMPE: *The Kiss Accepted and Returned*
16 April. Little Theatre, Haymarket
'Operetta'.[1] Text by James Ayres.

1745 G. F. HANDEL: *Hercules**
5 January. King's, Haymarket
Presented as an oratorio, but described as 'a musical drama'. English text by T. Broughton.

T. A. ARNE: *The Temple of Dullness**
17 January. Drury Lane
Comic opera. Text by Lewis Theobald. Two acts.

J. F. LAMPE: *Pyramus and Thisbe*
26 January. Covent Garden
Mock opera. One act. The overture and airs were published in full score.

T. A. ARNE: *The Picture, or, The Cuckold in Conceit*
11 February. Drury Lane
'Ballad opera'. Text by the Rev. James Miller, after Molière.

T. A. ARNE: *King Pepin's Campaign**
15 April. Drury Lane
Burlesque opera. Text by William Shirley. Two acts.

1746 ANON: *The Double Disappointment*
18 March. Drury Lane
Ballad opera. Text by Moses Mendez.

1747 WILLIAM BOYCE: *Peleus and Thetis**
29 April. London, Swan Tavern
Masque. Text by George Granville, Lord Lansdowne. One act. (This libretto was first set in 1701.)
  The manuscript score and parts are in the Bodleian Library, Oxford (Mus.d.24).

G. F. HANDEL: *Lucio Vero, Imperator di Roma**
14 November. King's, Haymarket
Pasticcio score, compiled mainly from Handel's operas. The text was presumably by Apostolo Zeno. Three acts.

(1) An early use of this term.

M. GREENE: *Phoebe**

'A pastoral opera'. Text by John Hoadly. Three acts. The autograph manuscript full score is in the Bodleian Library, Oxford (Mus.d.53). The music was composed in 1747; but the first performance, details of which are not known, may have taken place in 1748.

1749   T. A. ARNE: *The Triumph of Peace*
21 February. Drury Lane
Masque. Text by Robert Dodsley.

T. A. ARNE: *Henry and Emma, or, The Nut-brown Maid**

31 March. Covent Garden
'Musical Drama'. Text by the composer, based on Mathew Prior's poem 'The Nut-Brown Maid'.

W. BOYCE: *The Secular Masque**

July. Cambridge
Masque. Text by John Dryden. One act. (This libretto was first set by Daniel Purcell in 1700.)

   Boyce's music survives in an autograph manuscript full score at the Royal College of Music, London (93), for an all-male cast of altos, tenors, and basses.

W. BOYCE: *The Chaplet**

2 December. Drury Lane
'Musical entertainment'. Text by Moses Mendez. Two acts. The full score was published.

1750   T. A. ARNE: *Don Saverio**
15 February. Drury Lane
'Musical drama'. Text by the composer. Two acts.

CHARLES BURNEY: *Robin Hood*

13 December. Drury Lane
'A new musical entertainment'. Text by M. Mendez. Two acts. The title-page of the libretto says that the music was composed 'by the Society of the Temple of Apollo'.

1751   W. BOYCE: *The Shepherds' Lottery*
19 November. Drury Lane
'A musical entertainment'. Text by M. Mendez. Two parts. The full score was published.

1752   *In this year the English calendar changed to the modern Gregorian style. This meant that Wednesday, 2 September 1752, was followed by Thursday, 14 September 1752. All 17th century English dates (old style) will be found to be ten days behind the Gregorian style date. All 18th century English dates up to and including 2 September 1752 will be found to be eleven days behind the Gregorian style date.*[1]

(1) It should be noted that, for the sake of uniformity in international chronology, English dates up to and including 2 September 1752 have been adjusted in certain works of reference, *e.g.* Alfred Loewenberg's *Annals of Opera*.

1754 T. A. ARNE: *The Sheep-Shearing, or, Florizel and Perdita*
25 March. Covent Garden
'A pastoral comedy'. Text by McNamara Morgan, after Shakespeare.
Two acts.

T. A. ARNE: *Eliza*[(1)]
29 May. Little Theatre, Haymarket
'An English opera'. Text by Richard Rolt. Three acts. The full score was
published.

1755 J. C. SMITH: *The Fairies**
3 February. Drury Lane
Text by the composer, after Shakespeare. Prologue and three acts. The
full score was published.

T. A. ARNE: *Britannia**
May. Drury Lane
Masque. Text by David Mallet. One act.

1756 J. C. SMITH: *The Tempest**
11 February. Drury Lane
Text by David Garrick, after Shakespeare. Three acts. The full score was
published.

1759 T. A. ARNE: *The Sultan**
3 January. Covent Garden
Masque. Neither music nor libretto has survived.

1760 T. A. ARNE: *Thomas and Sally, or, The Sailor's Return**
28 November. Covent Garden
'A dramatic pastoral'. Text by Isaac Bickerstaffe. Two acts. The full score
was published.

J. C. SMITH: *The Enchanter, or, Love and Magic**
13 December. Drury Lane
Musical drama. Text by David Garrick. Two acts. The full score was
published.

1761 MICHAEL ARNE: *Edgar and Emmeline*
31 January. Drury Lane
'A fairy tale in a dramatic entertainment'. Text by John Hawkesworth.
Two acts.

J. STANLEY: *Arcadia, or, The Shepherd's Wedding**
26 October. Drury Lane
'A dramatic pastoral'. Text by Robert Lloyd. One act. The manuscript
full score is in the Royal College of Music, London (1022).

1762 ANON:[(2)] *Midas**
22 January. Dublin, Crow Street

(1) This opera is said to have been given first in Dublin.
(2) An analysis of the tunes borrowed is given by Roger Fiske in *English Theatre
Music in the Eighteenth Century*.

'English burletta'. Text by Kane O'Hara. Three acts. The original manuscripts of the libretto are in the National Library of Ireland, Dublin (MSS. 9249 and 9250).

T. A. ARNE: *Artaxerxes**
2 February. Covent Garden
'English opera'. Text by the composer, after Metastasio. Three acts. The full score was published.

T. A. ARNE and OTHERS: *Love in a Village*
8 December. Covent Garden
Pasticcio opera. Text by Isaac Bickerstaffe. Three acts.
   The score of this comic opera, which is an altered version of *The Village Opera* (1729), consists of a *pasticcio* of music by seventeen different composers, including Dr Thomas Arne himself. The manuscript of the full score is in the Royal College of Music, London (342). For the next half century or more, the *pasticcio* system flourished; and in the case of most of these *pasticcio* operas, the composer whose name is given primacy in this Register was also the editor and arranger of music culled from many different sources.

1763 ## PHILIP HAYES: *Telemachus**
10 May. Oxford Music School
Masque. Text by the Rev. George Graham. The manuscript full score is in the Bodleian Library, Oxford (Mus.d.77).

M. ARNE, J. BATTISHILL, C. BURNEY, J. C. SMITH: *A Fairy Tale**
26 November. Drury Lane
Afterpiece. Text by G. Colman (the elder), after Shakespeare. Two acts.

1764 ## M. ARNE: *Hymen**
20 January. Drury Lane
Afterpiece. Text by Allen. One act.

GEORGE RUSH: *The Royal Shepherd*[(1)]*
24 February. Drury Lane
'An English Opera'. Text by Richard Rolt, after Metastasio. Three acts.

CHARLES DIBDIN: *The Shepherd's Artifice**
21 May. Covent Garden
'A dramatic pastoral'. Written and composed by Dibdin at the age of nineteen. Two acts.

M. ARNE and J. BATTISHILL: *Almena**
2 November. Drury Lane
'An English Opera'. Text by Richard Rolt. Three acts.

G. RUSH: *The Capricious Lovers*
28 November. Drury Lane

(1) This was later cut down to two acts and adapted by Giuseppe Ferdinando Tenducci for production at Covent Garden on 15 December 1769 under the title of *Amintas*.

'A musical entertainment'. Text by Robert Lloyd. Two acts. Adapted from Favart's *Le caprice amoureux, ou, Ninette à la cour*.

T. A. ARNE: *The Guardian Outwitted*
12 December. Covent Garden
Comic opera. Text by the composer. Three acts.

1765 SAMUEL ARNOLD and OTHERS: *The Maid of the Mill*
31 January. Covent Garden
Pasticcio opera. Text by Isaac Bickerstaffe. Three acts.

WILLIAM BATES: *Pharnaces**
15 February. Drury Lane
Altered from the Italian (*viz.* Antonio Maria Lucchini's *Farnace*) by Thomas Hull.

WILLIAM YATES: *The Choice of Apollo**
11 March. Little Theatre, Haymarket
Masque. Text by John Potter. One act. The manuscript full score is in the Library of the Royal College of Music (645).

T. A. ARNE: *Olimpiade**
27 April. King's, Haymarket
Italian text by Metastasio. Three acts.

VARIOUS COMPOSERS: *Daphne and Amintor*
8 October. Drury Lane
Pasticcio opera. Text by Iasaac Bickerstaffe. Prologue and one act. Music drawn from Piccinni, Vento, Cocchi, Shalon, and Monsigny.

T. A. ARNE, S. ARNOLD and OTHERS: *The Summer's Tale*[(1)]
6 December. Covent Garden
Pasticcio opera. Text by Richard Cumberland. Three acts.

1767 M. ARNE: *Cymon*
2 January. Drury Lane
'A dramatic romance.' Text by David Garrick, after Dryden. Prologue, five acts, and epilogue.

C. DIBDIN and OTHERS: *Love in the City*[(2)]
21 February. Covent Garden
Pasticcio opera. Text by Isaac Bickerstaffe. Three acts.

S. ARNOLD: *Rosamond**
21 April. Covent Garden
After Addison's libretto. One act.

---

(1) This 'musical comedy' was later altered to make the two-act 'musical entertainment' *Amelia* (Drury Lane, 14 December 1771).
(2) Later on this became better known in an altered version as *The Romp*.

WILLIAM JACKSON: *Lycidas*
4 November. Covent Garden
'Musical entertainment'. Text by the composer, after Milton. One act.

THOMAS LINLEY: *The Royal Merchant*
14 December. Covent Garden
Text by Thomas Hull, after Beaumont and Fletcher. Three acts. (See also
The Camp, 1778.)

1768   **C. DIBDIN and OTHERS:** *Lionel and Clarissa*
25 February. Covent Garden
Comic opera. Text by Isaac Bickerstaffe. Three acts. (See also *The School
for Fathers*, 1770.)

F. H. BARTHELEMON: *Oithona**
3 March. Theatre Royal, Haymarket
'A dramatick poem'. Text after Ossian. Three acts.

F. H. BARTHELEMON: *The Judgment of Paris**
24 August. Theatre Royal, Haymarket
'English burletta'. Text by Ralph Schomberg. Two acts.

C. DIBDIN: *The Padlock*
3 October. Drury Lane
Comic opera. Text by Isaac Bickerstaffe. Two acts.

S. ARNOLD: *The Royal Garland**
10 October. Covent Garden
'A new occasional interlude'. Text by Isaac Bickerstaffe. One act.

C. DIBDIN: *Damon and Phillida*
21 December. Drury Lane
Comic opera. Text by the author, after Colley Cibber's *Love in a Riddle*
(1729). One act.

1769   **T. A. ARNE and OTHERS:** *Tom Jones*
14 January. Covent Garden
Pasticcio opera. Text by Joseph Reed, after Fielding. Three acts.

C. DIBDIN: *The Ephesian Matron**
12 May. Ranelagh Gardens
'A comic serenata'. Text by Isaac Bickerstaffe. One act. The recitatives
were published with the vocal score.

C. DIBDIN and OTHERS: *The Captive*
21 June. Theatre Royal, Haymarket
Pasticcio opera. Text by Isaac Bickerstaffe, after Dryden. Two acts.

G. RUSH and OTHERS: *Amintas**
15 December. Covent Garden
See *The Royal Shepherd* (1770).

1770 JOHN ABRAHAM FISHER: *The Court of Alexander**
5 January. Covent Garden
Burlesque. Text by George Alexander Stevens. Two acts.

C. DIBDIN and OTHERS: *The School for Fathers, or,*
Lionel and Clarissa
8 February. Drury Lane
Pasticcio opera. Text by Isaac Bickerstaffe. Three acts. An alteration of
Lionel and Clarissa (1768).

T. A. ARNE and WILLIAM BATES: *The Ladies' Frolick*
7 May. Drury Lane.
An alteration of *The Jovial Crew* (1731). The libretto was altered by
James Love; and there were new numbers by T. A. Arne and W. Bates.
About a dozen of the original airs were kept.

C. DIBDIN: *The Recruiting Serjeant**
20 July. Ranelagh Gardens
'A musical entertainment'. Text by Isaac Bickerstaffe. One act. The full
score was published in 1776. 'I published the Music on my own account,'
said Dibdin, 'and found it unsuccessful.'[1]

S. ARNOLD: *The Revenge**
Marylebone Gardens
'A burletta'. Text by Thomas Chatterton. Two acts.
   Although this work appears to have been put into rehearsal in the
summer of 1770, just before Chatterton's death, there is no record of its
actual performance.

S. ARNOLD: *The Portrait**
22 November. Covent Garden
Burletta. Text by George Colman (the elder) after Grétry's *Le Tableau*
parlant.

1771 JAMES HOOK: *Dido*
24 July. Theatre Royal, Haymarket
Comic opera. Text by Thomas Bridges. Two acts.

T. A. ARNE: *The Fairy Prince**
12 November. Covent Garden
Masque. Text by George Colman (the elder) after Ben Jonson's *Oberon*
(1611). Three acts.

T. A. ARNE and OTHERS: *Amelia*
14 December. Drury Lane
See *The Summer's Tale* (1765).

1772 T. A. ARNE: *The Cooper*
10 June. Theatre Royal, Haymarket
'A musical entertainment'. Text by the composer. Two acts.

(1) From *The Musical Tour of Mr Dibdin*, 1788. *op. cit.*

T. A. ARNE: *Elfrida*
21 November. Covent Garden
'A dramatic poem'. Text by William Mason. Five acts.

T. A. ARNE: *The Rose*
2 December. Drury Lane
Comic opera. Text by the composer. Two acts

1773　### C. DIBDIN: *The Wedding Ring*
1 February. Drury Lane
Comic opera. Text by the composer, after Goldoni's *Il Filosofo di Campagna*. Two acts.

T. A. ARNE and OTHERS: *The Golden Pippin**
6 February. Covent Garden
'An English burletta'. Text by Kane O'Hara. Three acts.

C. DIBDIN: *The Trip to Portsmouth*
11 August. Theatre Royal, Haymarket
'A comic sketch'. Text by G. A. Stevens. One act.

C. DIBDIN: *The Deserter*
2 November. Drury Lane
'A new musical drama'. Text by the composer, after Sedaine. Two acts. An adaptation of Monsigny's *Le Déserteur*.

T. A. ARNE: *Achilles in Petticoats*
16 December. Covent Garden
'An opera' (title-page). Text by George Colman (the elder), after John Gay's *Achilles* (1733). Two acts.

C. DIBDIN: *A Christmas Tale*
27 December. Drury Lane
'A new dramatic entertainment'. Text by David Garrick. Five parts.

1774　### C. DIBDIN: *The Waterman, or, The First of August*
8 August. Theatre Royal, Haymarket
'Ballad opera' (title-page) or 'ballad farce' (preface). Text by the composer. Two acts.

F. H. BARTHELEMON and OTHERS: *The Maid of the Oaks*
5 November. Drury Lane
'Dramatic entertainment'. Text by Lieutenant-General John Burgoyne. Five acts.
　　A shorter version in the form of a masque had been played at The Oaks, Lord Derby's seat near Epsom, in June 1774.

C. DIBDIN: *The Cobler, or, A Wife of Ten Thousand*
9 December. Drury Lane
Ballad opera. Text by composer. Two acts.

1775 C. DIBDIN and OTHERS: *The Two Misers*
21 *January*. Covent Garden
Musical farce. Text by Kane O'Hara, after F. de Falbaire's *Les deux avares* (music by Grétry). Two acts.

THOMAS CARTER: *The Rival Candidates*
1 *February*. Drury Lane
Comic opera. Text by the Rev. Henry Bate (later Sir Henry Bate Dudley). Two acts and epilogue.

C. DIBDIN: *The Quaker*
3 *May*. Drury Lane
Comic opera. Text by the composer. Two acts.
  The actor Brereton bought this opera, words and music, from Dibdin for £70 and, though he played no part in it, chose it for his benefit night at Drury Lane. He then sold it for £100 to David Garrick, who forgot about it. After Garrick's retirement, Linley (the elder) revived it at Drury Lane on 7 October 1777.

W. BATES: *The Theatrical Candidates*
23 *September*. Drury Lane
'A musical prelude'. Text by David Garrick. One act. This piece was written and performed 'upon the opening and alterations of the theatre'.

T. A. ARNE: *May-Day, or, The Little Gipsy*
28 *October*. Drury Lane
'A musical farce'. Text by David Garrick. One act.

THOMAS LINLEY (the elder and the younger) and OTHERS: *The Duenna, or, The Double Elopement*
21 *November*. Covent Garden
Pasticcio comic opera. Text by R. B. Sheridan. Three acts. The Linleys contributed about fifteen musical numbers; and there were other numbers by Michael Arne, Galliard, Giordani, William Hayes, Jackson, Rauzzini, and Sacchini. The manuscript full score of the numbers contributed by T. Linley (the younger) is in the British Library (Egerton 2493) and of Act III in the Gresham College Library in the City of London Guildhall.
  It was revived by Nigel Playfair at the Lyric Theatre, Hammersmith, on 23 October 1924 with the music arranged by Alfred Reynolds.
  A new edition of the full score was made by Roger Fiske and presented by Opera da Camera at the Collegiate Theatre, London, on 16 March 1976 as part of the Camden Music Festival.

1776 C. DIBDIN: *The Blackamoor wash'd White*
1 *February*. Drury Lane
Comic opera. Text by the Rev. Henry Bate (later Sir Henry Bate Dudley).

C. DIBDIN: *The Metamorphoses*
26 *August*. Theatre Royal, Haymarket
Comic opera. Text by the composer.

C. DIBDIN and OTHERS: *The Seraglio*
14 November. Covent Garden
Comic opera. Text by the composer. Two acts.

T. LINLEY (the elder): *Selim and Azor*
5 December. Drury Lane
Translated from the French of Marmontel by Sir George Collier. (The original opera by Gretry appeared in 1771.)

1777   T. CARTER: *The Milesian*
20 March. Drury Lane
Comic opera. Text by Isaac Jackman. Two acts.

S. ARNOLD: *April-Day*
22 August. Theatre Royal, Haymarket
Burletta. Text by Kane O'Hara. Three acts.

T. A. ARNE, A. M. G. SACCHINI, J. A. FISHER: *Love Finds the Way*
18 November. Covent Garden
Comic opera. Text by Thomas Hull, after A. Murphy's *The School for Guardians*. Three acts.

1778   C. DIBDIN: *Poor Vulcan*
4 February. Covent Garden
Burletta. Text by the composer. Two acts. The score contains one air each by T. A. Arne and S. Arnold.

T. LINLEY (the younger): *The Cady of Bagdad*
19 February. Drury Lane
Comic opera. Text by Abraham Portal. The manuscript full score is in the British Library (Add. MS. 29297).

PHILIP COGAN: *The Ruling Passion*
24 February. Dublin, Capel Street
Comic opera. Text by Leonard MacNally.

WILLIAM SHIELD: *The Flitch of Bacon*
17 August. Theatre Royal, Haymarket
Comic opera. Text by the Rev. Henry Bate (later Sir Henry Bate Dudley). Two acts. According to Michael Kelly (*Reminiscences*, 1826) the rondo 'Io ti lascio, e questo addio' from Schuster's setting of Metastasio's *La Didone Abbandonata* (1776) was introduced by Shield into this comic opera to the words 'No, 'twas neither shape nor feature'.

C. DIBDIN: *Rose and Colin*
18 September. Covent Garden
Comic opera. Text by the composer. One act.

C. DIBDIN: *The Wives Revenged*
18 September. Covent Garden
Comic opera. Text by the composer. One act.

C. DIBDIN: *Annette and Lubin*
2 October. Covent Garden
Comic opera. Text by the composer. One act. An alteration of Benoît Blaise's *Annette et Lubin* (1762).

T. LINLEY (the elder): *The Camp*
15 October. Drury Lane
'A musical entertainment'. Text attributed to R. B. Sheridan and Richard Tickell. Two acts. Many of the numbers in *The Camp* were taken from Linley's score for *The Royal Merchant* (1767).

JAMES HOOK: *The Lady of the Manor*
23 November. Covent Garden
Comic opera. Text by William Kenrick, after Charles Johnson's *Country Lasses*. Three acts.

1779 ### W. SHIELD and OTHERS: *The Cobler of Castlebury*
27 April. Covent Garden
'A musical entertainment'. Text by Charles Stuart. Two acts.

C. DIBDIN: *The Chelsea Pensioner*
6 May. Covent Garden
Comic opera. Text by the composer. Two acts.

S. ARNOLD and OTHERS: *Summer Amusement, or, An Adventure at Margate*
1 July. Theatre Royal, Haymarket
Comic opera. Text by Miles Peter Andrews and William Augustus Miles. Three acts.

S. ARNOLD: *The Son-in-Law*
14 August. Theatre Royal, Haymarket
Comic opera. Text by John O'Keeffe. Two acts.

1780 ### C. DIBDIN: *The Shepherdess of the Alps*
18 January. Covent Garden
Comic opera. Text by the composer. Three acts.

THOMAS BUTLER: *The Widow of Delphi, or, The Descent of the Deities*
1 February. Covent Garden
'A musical drama'. Text by Richard Cumberland.

M. ARNE: *The Artifice*
14 April. Drury Lane
Comic opera. Text by William Augustus Miles. Two acts.

W. SHIELD and OTHERS: *The Siege of Gibraltar*
25 April. Covent Garden
'Musical farce'. Text by Frederick Pilon. Two acts.

S. ARNOLD: *Fire and Water!*
8 July. Theatre Royal, Haymarket
Comic opera. Text by Miles Peter Andrews. Two acts.

C. DIBDIN: *The Islanders*
25 November. Covent Garden
Comic opera. Text by the composer. Three acts.

W. JACKSON: *The Lord of the Manor*
27 December. Drury Lane
Comic opera. Text by John Burgoyne, after Marmontel. Three acts. The full score was published.

1781   ### S. ARNOLD: *The Dead Alive*
16 June. Theatre Royal, Haymarket
Comic opera. Text by John O'Keeffe. Two acts.

S. ARNOLD: *The Agreeable Surprise*
3 September. Theatre Royal, Haymarket
Comic opera. Text by John O'Keeffe. Two acts.

C. DIBDIN: *Jupiter and Alcmena*
27 October. Covent Garden
Burlesque opera. Text by the composer. Three acts.

S. ARNOLD: *The Banditti, or, Love's Labyrinth*
28 November. Covent Garden
Comic opera. Text by John O'Keeffe. Two acts.
   Later revived as *The Castle of Andalusia* in three acts (1782).

1782   ### WILLIAM BECKFORD: *The Arcadian Pastoral*
13 April. London, Queensberry House
Pastoral opera. Text by Elizabeth Craven. Five acts.
   This pastoral was retitled *The Descent of Belinda* when the B.B.C. revived it for a radio broadcast on 13 February 1955. The date here given for the first performance is that of the dress rehearsal. The spoken dialogue is lost; but the manuscript score has been preserved with the Hamilton papers in Edinburgh.

P. COGAN and SIR JOHN STEVENSON: *The Contract*
14 May. Dublin, Smock Alley
Comic opera. Text by Robert Houlton.

T. CARTER: *The Fair American*
18 May. Drury Lane
Comic opera. Text by Frederick Pilon. Three acts.

S. ARNOLD: *The Castle of Andalusia*
2 November. Covent Garden
Comic opera. An alteration of *The Banditti* (1781).

W. SHIELD and OTHERS: *Rosina*
31 December. Covent Garden

Comic opera. Text by Frances Brooke, after Favart. Two acts. The manuscript full score is in the British Library (Add. MS. 33815).

1783 W. SHIELD: *The Shamrock, or, The Anniversary of St Patrick*
7 April. Covent Garden
Comic opera. Text by John O'Keeffe. Two acts.
   An earlier version was given at Crow Street Theatre, Dublin, on 15 April 1777, though it is uncertain whether this was presented as an opera or a straight play.
   Revived at Covent Garden (4 November 1783) in an altered version as *The Poor Soldier*.

S. ARNOLD and OTHERS: *The Birth-Day, or, The Prince of Arragon*
12 August. Theatre Royal, Haymarket
'A dramatick piece, with songs'. Text by John O'Keeffe. Two acts.

S. ARNOLD and OTHERS: *Gretna Green*
28 August. Theatre Royal, Haymarket
Comic opera. Text by Charles Stuart. Two acts. The music of this pasticcio consists mainly of 'Italian, French, Irish, English and Scotch music'. There are two numbers by Giordani, and only one number (in addition to the overture) composed by Arnold.

W. JACKSON: *The Metamorphosis*
5 December. Drury Lane
Comic opera. Text by the composer.

1784 W. SHIELD and OTHERS: *Robin Hood, or, Sherwood Forest*
17 April. Covent Garden
Comic opera. Text by Leonard MacNally. Three acts.

S. ARNOLD and OTHERS: *Two to One*
19 June. Theatre Royal, Haymarket
Comic opera. Text by George Colman (the younger). Three acts.

W. SHIELD and OTHERS: *The Noble Peasant*
2 August. Theatre Royal, Haymarket
Comic opera. Text by Thomas Holcroft. Three acts.

S. ARNOLD: *Peeping Tom of Coventry*
6 September. Theatre Royal, Haymarket
Comic opera. Text by John O'Keeffe. Two acts.

T. LINLEY (the elder): *The Spanish Rivals*
4 November. Drury Lane
Musical farce. Text by Mark Lonsdale. Two acts.

W. SHIELD and OTHERS: *Fontainebleau, or, Our Way in France*
16 November. Covent Garden
Comic opera. Text by John O'Keeffe. Three acts.

1785   C. DIBDIN: *Liberty-Hall*
8 February. Drury Lane
Comic opera. Text by the composer. Two acts.

W. SHIELD: *The Nunnery*
12 April. Covent Garden
Text by William Pearce. Two acts.

STEPHEN STORACE: *Gli Sposi Malcontenti*
1 June. Vienna, Burgtheater
Italian text by Gaetano Brunati. Two acts. A manuscript copy of the full
score has been preserved in the Sächsisches Landeshauptarchiv; Dresden
(Mus. 4109/F/2).

W. SHIELD: *The Choleric Fathers*
10 November. Covent Garden
Comic opera. Text by Thomas Holcroft. Three acts.

T. LINLEY (the elder): *The Strangers at Home*
8 December. Drury Lane
Comic opera. Text by James Cobb. Three acts.
   An abridged version entitled *The Algerine Slaves* was produced in 1792.

1786   W. SHIELD: *Patrick in Prussia, or, Love in a Camp*
17 February. Covent Garden
Comic opera. Text by John O'Keeffe. Two acts.
   A sequel to *The Shamrock* (1783) and *The Poor Soldier* (1783).

J. HOOK: *The Fair Peruvian*
18 March. Covent Garden
Comic opera. English text adapted from Favart's *L'amitié à l'épreuve*
(1770) with music by Gretry.
   Sometimes referred to as *The Peruvian*.

C. DIBDIN: *A Match for a Widow, or, The Frolics of Fancy*
17 April. Dublin, Smock Alley
Comic opera. Text by Joseph Atkinson, after Patrat's *L'heureuse erreur*.
Three acts.
   This comic opera introduces a Yankee character (Jonathan) who sings a
song to the tune of *Yankee doodle*.[1]

S. ARNOLD: *The Siege of Curzola*
12 August. Theatre Royal, Haymarket
Comic opera. Text by John O'Keeffe. Three acts.

S. STORACE: *Gli Equivoci*
27 December. Vienna, Burgtheater

(1) It should be noted that the tune of *Yankee doodle* had already been specified
for one of the airs ('O! how joyful shall I be, When I get de money') in Andrew
Barton's American ballad opera *The Disappointment* (1767) which was put into
rehearsal in Philadelphia, but never performed.

'Dramma buffo'. Italian text by Lorenzo da Ponte, founded on Shakespeare's *Comedy of Errors*. Two acts. A copy of the full score has been preserved in the Sächsische Landeshauptarchiv, Dresden (Mus. 4109/f/1).

The first English performance was given by Opera da Camera on 20 February 1974 at the Collegiate Theatre, London, in the course of the Camden Festival in a version edited by Richard Platt with an English translation of the libretto by Arthur Jacobs.

1787   C. DIBDIN: *Harvest Home*
16 May. Theatre Royal, Haymarket
Comic opera. Text by the composer. Two acts.

S. ARNOLD: *Inkle and Yarico*
4 August. Theatre Royal, Haymarket
Comic opera. Text by George Colman (the younger). Three acts.

W. SHIELD: *The Farmer*
31 October. Covent Garden
Comic opera. Text by John O'Keeffe. Two acts.

1788   ANON: *Jamie and Bess, or, The Laird in Disguise*
12 January. Edinburgh
Ballad opera. Text by Andrew Shirrefs, in imitation of *The Gentle Shepherd* (1729).

T. LINLEY (the elder): *Love in the East, or, Adventures of Twelve Hours*
25 February. Drury Lane
Comic opera. Text by James Cobb. Three acts.

S. STORACE: *La Cameriera Astuta*
4 March. King's, Haymarket
Comic opera. Author of the Italian text unknown. Two acts.

W. SHIELD: *Marian*
22 May. Covent Garden
Comic opera. Text by Frances Brooke. Two acts.

S. STORACE and OTHERS: *The Doctor and the Apothecary*
25 October. Drury Lane
'Musical entertainment'. Text by J. Cobb. Two acts. Adapted by Storace from Ditters von Dittersdorf's 'singspiel' *Der Apotheker und der Doktor* (Vienna, 1786). One of the numbers is by Paisiello.

W. SHIELD: *The Highland Reel*
6 November. Covent Garden
Comic opera. Text by John O'Keeffe. Three acts.

1789   S. ARNOLD: *The Battle of Hexham, or, Days of Old*
11 August. Theatre Royal, Haymarket
Comic opera. Text by George Colman (the younger). Three acts.

THOMAS SHAW and OTHERS: *The Island of St Marguerite*
13 November. Drury Lane
'An opera'. Text by the Hon. John St John, after Voltaire's story of the Man in the Iron Mask. Two acts.

S. STORACE and OTHERS: *The Haunted Tower*
24 November. Drury Lane
Comic opera. Text by James Cobb. Three acts. The score included numbers by Linley, Martini, Paisiello, Pleyel, and Sarti.

1790 JOSEPH QUESNEL: *Colas et Colinette*
14 January. Montreal
French text of this comic opera in the style of a 'comédie mêlée d'ariettes' by the composer. Revived in Quebec on 29 January 1805.

W. SHIELD: *The Czar*
8 March. Covent Garden
Comic opera. Text by John O'Keeffe. Three acts. Also known as *The Czar Peter*.

S. STORACE and OTHERS: *No Song, No Supper*
16 April. Drury Lane
An opera'. Text by Prince Hoare. Two acts.
   Storace utilised some of his music from *Gli Equivoci* (1786) for this opera. The score included numbers by Grétry, Harington, and Pleyel. A copyist's manuscript of the full score is in the Library of the Royal College of Music (597).

S. ARNOLD: *New Spain, or, Love in Mexico*
16 July. Theatre Royal, Haymarket
'An opera'. Text by John Scawen. Three acts.

1791 S. STORACE and OTHERS: *The Siege of Belgrade*
1 January. Drury Lane
Comic opera. Text by James Cobb. Three acts. The score included numbers by Kelly, Paisiello, Salieri, and Martin y Soler.
   See also *Catherine* (1830).

W. SHIELD: *The Woodman*
26 February. Covent Garden
Comic opera. Text by Sir Henry Bate Dudley. Three acts.

S. STORACE and OTHERS: *The Cave of Trophonius*
3 May. Drury Lane
'An opera'. Text by Prince Hoare, after Giambattista Casti. Two acts. Adapted from the opera by Salieri.

S. ARNOLD: *The Surrender of Calais*
30 July. Theatre Royal, Haymarket
'A play'. Text by George Colman (the younger). Three acts.

W. SHIELD and WILLIAM REEVE: *Oscar and Malvina, or, The Hall of Fingal*
20 *October*. Covent Garden
'Ballet pantomime (taken from Ossian)' Reeve completed Shield's unfinished score.

1792 T. LINLEY (the elder): *The Algerine Slaves*
17 *March*. King's, Haymarket
An abridged version of *The Strangers at Home* (1785).

THOMAS CARTER: *Just in Time*
10 *May*. Covent Garden
Comic opera. Text by Thomas Hurlstone. Three acts.

S. STORACE and OTHERS: *Dido, Queen of Carthage**
23 *May*. King's, Haymarket
Opera 'with the Masque of Neptune's Prophecy'. Text by Prince Hoare, after Metastasio. Presented by the Drury Lane Company. The score included numbers by Sacchini, Salieri, and Sarti.

W. SHIELD and OTHERS: *Hartford-Bridge, or, The Skirts of the Camp*
3 *November*. Covent Garden
'Operatic farce'. Text by William Pearce. Two acts.

S. STORACE and OTHERS: *The Pirates*
21 *November*. King's, Haymarket
'An opera'. Text by James Cobb. Three acts. Presented by the Drury Lane Company. The score included numbers by Anfossi, Bianchi, and Guglielmi.
 See also *Isidore de Merida* (1827).

1793 W. SHIELD and OTHERS: *The Midnight Wanderers*
25 *February*. Covent Garden
Comic opera. Text by W. Pearce. Two acts.

S. STORACE and OTHERS: *Le Nozze di Dorina*
26 *February*. King's, Haymarket
'Comic opera'. Italian text after Goldoni. Two acts.
 Giuseppe Sarti's opera *Fra due Litiganti il terzo gode, ossia, I Pretendenti delusi* was first produced at the Scala, Milan, in 1782. The first performance in England was at the King's Theatre (6 January 1784) as *I Rivali delusi*. The text was later altered for this version (*Le Nozze di Dorina*), and Sarti's score edited by Storace, who added numbers by himself and by Martin y Soler.

THOMAS ATTWOOD: *Ozmyn and Daraxa*
7 *March*. King's, Haymarket
'Musical romance'. Text by James Boaden. Presented by the Drury Lane Company.

S. STORACE: *The Prize, or, 2, 5, 3, 8*
11 *March*. King's, Haymarket

'Musical farce'. Text by Prince Hoare. Two acts. Presented by the Drury Lane Company.

Capt. WARNER: *The Armourer*
4 April. Covent Garden
Comic opera. Text by Richard Cumberland.

T. ATTWOOD and OTHERS: *The Mariners*
10 May. King's, Haymarket
'A musical entertainment'. Text by Samuel Birch. Two acts. Presented by the Drury Lane Company.

W. SHIELD and OTHERS: *Sprigs of Laurel*
11 May. Covent Garden
Comic opera. Text by John O'Keeffe. Two acts.
   Later revived in an altered version as *The Rival Soldiers* (1797).

S. ARNOLD: *The Mountaineers*
3 August. Theatre Royal, Haymarket
'A play'. Text by George Colman (the younger). Three acts.

T. ATTWOOD: *Caernarvon Castle, or, The Birth of the Prince of Wales*
12 August. Theatre Royal, Haymarket
'An opera'. Text by the Rev. John Rose. Two acts.

S. ARNOLD: *The Children in the Wood*
1 October. Theatre Royal, Haymarket
'A musical piece'. Text by Prince Hoare. Two acts. Presented by the Drury Lane Company.

S. STORACE: *My Grandmother*
16 December. Theatre Royal, Haymarket
'A musical farce'. Text by Prince Hoare. Two acts. Presented by the Drury Lane Company.

1794   ## W. REEVE: *The Purse, or, Benevolent Tar*
8 February. Theatre Royal, Haymarket
'A musical drama'. Text by James C. Cross. One act. Presented by the Drury Lane Company.

W. SHIELD and OTHERS: *The Travellers in Switzerland*
22 [or 25] February. Covent Garden
Comic opera. Text by Sir Henry Bate Dudley. Three acts.

W. SHIELD and OTHERS: *Netley Abbey*
10 April. Covent Garden
'An operatic farce'. Text by William Pearce. Two acts. This pasticcio contained numbers by Baumgarten, Parke, Paisiello, and Howard, in addition to Shield.

W. REEVE: *British Fortitude, and Hibernian Friendship, or, An Escape from France*
29 April. Covent Garden
'Musical Drama'. Text by James C. Cross. One act.

W. REEVE: *The Sicilian Romance, or, The Apparition of the Cliffs*
28 May. Covent Garden
'An opera'. Text by Henry Siddons. Three acts.

S. STORACE and OTHERS: *Lodoiska*
9 June. Drury Lane
Sometimes described as 'an opera' and sometimes as 'a musical romance'.
Text by John Philip Kemble. Three acts. The score included numbers by
Cherubini, Kreutzer, and Andreozzi.

S. STORACE, MICHAEL KELLY and OTHERS: *The Glorious First of June*
2 July. Drury Lane
'A new and appropriate entertainment . . . Given for the benefit of the
Widows and Orphans of the Brave Men who fell in the late Engagements
under Lord Howe'. Michael Kelly says (in his *Reminiscences*, 1826, *op. cit.*) 'Storace and myself gave it some new songs; but the music was chiefly old'.
   An altered version was produced at Drury Lane in 1797 under the title
of *Cape St Vincent, or, British Valour Triumphant.*

S. ARNOLD: *Auld Robin Gray*
29 July. Theatre Royal, Haymarket
'A pastoral entertainment'. Text by Samuel James Arnold. Two acts.

W. REEVE: *The Apparition*
3 September. Theatre Royal, Haymarket
'A musical dramatic romance'. Text by James C. Cross. Two acts.

W. SHIELD: *Arrived at Portsmouth*
30 October. Covent Garden
'An operatic drama'. Text by William Pearce. Two acts.

S. STORACE: *The Cherokee*
20 December. Drury Lane
'An opera'. Text by James Cobb. Three acts.
   For a later adaptation, see *Algonah* (1802).

1795 **J. P. SALOMON and R. SPOFFORTH:** *Windsor Castle, or, The Fair Maid of Kent*
6 April. Covent Garden
'An opera'. Text by William Pearce. Two acts. Performed in honour of
the marriage of the Prince and Princess of Wales. The second act
contained a masque entitled *The Marriage of Peleus and Thetis*. The
overture was composed expressly for the occasion by Joseph Haydn, who
was in London at the time.

W. SHIELD: *The Irish Mimic, or, Blunders at Brighton*
23 April. Covent Garden
'A musical entertainment'. Text by John O'Keeffe. Two acts.

T. ATTWOOD: *The Adopted Child*
1 May. Drury Lane
'A musical drama'. Text by Samuel Birch. Two acts.

T. ATTWOOD: *The Poor Sailor, or, Little Ben and Little Bob*
29 May. Covent Garden
Author of the text unknown.

S. STORACE: *The Three and the Deuce*
2 September. Theatre Royal, Haymarket
'A comic drama'. Text by Prince Hoare.

1796   W. SHIELD: *Lock and Key*
2 February. Covent Garden
'A musical entertainment'. Text by Prince Hoare. Two acts. The overture was composed by W. T. Parke.

S. STORACE: *The Iron Chest*
12 March. Drury Lane
'A play'. Text by George Colman (the younger). Three acts.

T. ATTWOOD: *The Smugglers*
13 April. Drury Lane
'A musical drama'. Text by Samuel Birch. Two acts.

W. SHIELD: *The Wicklow Gold Mines, or, The Lads of the Hills*
13 April. Covent Garden
'Opera'. Text by John O'Keeffe. Three acts.
   Later the same year it was given under the title of *The Wicklow Mountains*.

S. STORACE and OTHERS: *Mahmoud*
30 April. Drury Lane
'A musical romance'. Text by Prince Hoare. Three acts. The score included numbers by Paisiello, Haydn, and Sarti.

W. REEVE: *The Charity Boy*
5 November. Drury Lane
'A musical entertainment'. Text by James C. Cross.

W. SHIELD: *Abroad and at Home*
19 November. Covent Garden
Comic opera. Text by Joseph George Holman. Three acts.

S. ARNOLD: *The Shipwreck*
19 December. Drury Lane
Comic opera. Text by S. J. Arnold.

1797   WILLIAM LINLEY: *The Honey Moon*
7 January. Drury Lane
Comic opera. Text by the composer.

MICHAEL KELLY: *A Friend in Need*
9 February. Drury Lane
'A musical entertainment' (Kelly). Text by Prince Hoare.
   In his *Reminiscences* (published in 1826) Kelly listed sixty-two theatrical
pieces for which he had composed incidental music. He termed only one of
these an 'opera' *viz. The Unknown Guest* (1815); but it seems reasonable to
suppose that some of the others approximated to the condition of 'comic
operas' at that time. Where possible, Kelly's own description of the type of
theatrical piece has been given within inverted commas.

S. STORACE and OTHERS: *Cape St Vincent, or, British
Valour Triumphant*
March. Drury Lane
An alteration of *The Glorious First of June* (1794).

W. SHIELD: *The Italian Villagers*
25 April. Covent Garden

W. SHIELD and OTHERS: *The Rival Soldiers*
17 May. Covent Garden
An altered version of *Sprigs of Laurel* (1793).

1798   M. KELLY: *Blue-Beard, or, Female Curiosity!*
16 January. Drury Lane
'A dramatick romance' (Kelly). Text by George Colman (the younger).
Two acts.

W. REEVE: *The Raft, or, Both Sides of the Water*
31 March. Covent Garden
'A musical drama'. Text by James C. Cross. One act.

S. ARNOLD: *Throw Physic to the Dogs!*
6 July. Theatre Royal, Haymarket
'Musical Farce'. Text by H. Lee. Two acts.

S. ARNOLD: *Cambro-Britons*
21 July. Theatre Royal, Haymarket
'Historical play'. Text by James Boaden. Three acts. The words of two of
the songs were written by George Colman (the younger).

T. ATTWOOD: *The Mouth of the Nile, or, The Glorious
First of August*
25 October. Covent Garden
'A musical entertainment'. Text by T. J. Dibdin. One act.

JOSEPH MAZZINGHI and W. REEVE: *Ramah Droog,
or, Wine does Wonders*
12 November. Covent Garden
Comic opera. Text by James Cobb. Three acts.

J. L. DUSSEK and M. KELLY: *The Captive of Spilburg*
14 November. Drury Lane
Text by Prince Hoare. 'The next musical piece I produced at Drury Lane, was in conjunction with Mr Dusseck, the celebrated piano-forte player; he composed the serious part of it—I the comic'.—*Reminiscences of Michael Kelly* (1826).
   This piece was adapted from Marsollier's *Camille, ou, Le Souterrain*.

1799   SIR JOHN STEVENSON: *Love in a Blaze*
29 May. Dublin, Crow Street
Comic opera. Text by Joseph Atkinson.

T. ATTWOOD: *The Castle of Sorrento*
17 July. Theatre Royal, Haymarket
Comic opera. Text by Henry Heartwell and George Colman (the younger), after the French opera *Le Prisonnier* (music by Della Maria). Two acts.

T. ATTWOOD: *The Red-Cross Knights*
21 August. Theatre Royal, Haymarket
Text by J. G. Holman, after *Die Räuber* by Schiller. The score included a number from Mozart's *Die Zauberflöte*.

JOHN MOORHEAD: *The Naval Pillar*
7 October. Covent Garden
'Musical entertainment'. Text by T. J. Dibdin.

J. MAZZINGHI and W. REEVE: *The Turnpike Gate*
14 November. Covent Garden
'Musical entertainment'. Text by Thomas Knight. Two acts.

W. LINLEY: *The Pavilion*
16 November. Drury Lane
'Musical entertainment'. Text by the composer. The manuscript full score is in the British Library (Egerton 2494).
   Subsequently it seems to have been played under the title of *The Ring*.

1800   M. KELLY: *Of Age Tomorrow*
1 February. Drury Lane
Operatic farce. Text by T. J. Dibdin, after the German of Kotzebue.

FLORIO: *The Egyptian Festival*
11 March. Drury Lane
Opera. Text by Andrew Franklin. Three acts.

J. MAZZINGHI and W. REEVE: *Paul and Virginia*
1 May. Covent Garden
Comic opera. Text by J. Cobb. One act.

EARL OF MOUNT EDGCUMBE: *Zenobia**
22 May. King's, Haymarket
Italian text by Metastasio.

JOHN DAVY: *What a Blunder!*
14 August. Theatre Royal, Haymarket
Comic opera. Text by J. G. Holman. Three acts.

JAMES HOOK: *Wilmore Castle*
21 October. Drury Lane
Comic opera. Text by R. Houlton. Two acts.

S. ARNOLD: *Virginia*
30 October. Drury Lane
Text by Mrs Frances Plowden.

T. ATTWOOD and J. MOORHEAD: *Il Bondocani, or,
The Caliph Robber*
15 November. Covent Garden
Comic opera. Text by T. J. Dibdin. Three acts. The score contained a
number from Mozart's *Die Entführung aus dem Serail.*

1801 J. MAZZINGHI and W. REEVE: *The Blind Girl, or, A
Receipt for Beauty*
22 April. Covent Garden
Comic opera. Text by Thomas Morton.

SIR JOHN STEVENSON: *The Bedouins, or, The Arabs of
the Desert*
1 May. Dublin, Crow Street
Comic opera. Text by Eyles Irwin.

M. KELLY: *Adelmorn the Outlaw*
4 May. Drury Lane
Musical 'drama' (Kelly). Text by Matthew Gregory Lewis.

T. ATTWOOD: *The Sea-Side Story*
12 May. Covent Garden
Comic opera. Text by William Dimond.

M. KELLY: *The Gipsey Prince*
24 July. Theatre Royal, Haymarket
'Musical afterpiece' (Kelly). Text by Thomas Moore.

J. MAZZINGHI and W. REEVE: *Chains of the Heart, or,
The Slave by Choice*
9 December. Covent Garden
Comic opera. Text by Prince Hoare.

1802 W. REEVE, J. MOORHEAD, J. DAVY, M. CORRI, and
J. BRAHAM: *The Cabinet*
9 February. Covent Garden
Comic opera. Text by T. J. Dibdin. Three acts.

M. KELLY: *Algonah*
30 April. Drury Lane
An adaptation of his own *Cherokee* (1794) by James Cobb. The music seems to have been recomposed by Kelly.

J. DAVY: *The Caffres, or, Buried Alive*
2 June. Covent Garden
Text by E. J. Eyre.

W. REEVE, J. MOORHEAD, J. DAVY, M. CORRI, and J. BRAHAM: *Family Quarrels*
18 December. Covent Garden
Comic opera. Text by T. J. Dibdin.

1803 ### M. KELLY: *The Hero of the North*
19 February. Drury Lane
'An historical musical drama' (Kelly). Text by W. Dimond.

W. REEVE: *Edward and Susan, or, The Beauty of Buttermere*
11 April. Sadler's Wells
'An operatic piece in rhyme'.[1] Text by Charles Dibdin the younger. (This is referred to by William Wordsworth in Book VII of *The Prelude*.)

W. REEVE: *The Caravan, or, The Driver and his Dog*
5 December. Drury Lane
Text by Frederic Reynolds.

J. BRAHAM: *The English Fleet in 1342*
13 December. Covent Garden
'An historical comic opera'. Text by T. J. Dibdin. Three acts.

1804 ### J. BRAHAM: *The Paragraph*
8 March. Covent Garden
Text by Prince Hoare.

W. REEVE: *The Little Gipsies*
2 April. Sadler's Wells
Text by Charles Dibdin the younger.
   Early in the 19th century Charles Dibdin the younger became proprietor of Sadler's Wells and wrote innumerable pieces, burlettas, pantomimes, spectacles &c. for that theatre. In his *Professional and Literary Memoirs*[2] he refers to *The Little Gipsies* under the title of *The two little Gipsies* as 'an operatic Piece, taken from the same Spanish Story on which *Preciosa* (lately performed at Covent Garden with Weber's Music) was founded.'

(1) From *Professional and Literary Memoirs of Charles Dibdin the Younger: Dramatist and Upward of Thirty Years Manager of Minor Theatres* (ed. George Speaight). London, Society for Theatre Research, 1956.
(2) *ibid*.

M. KELLY: *The Hunter of the Alps*
3 July. Theatre Royal, Haymarket
'A musical piece' (Kelly). Text by W. Dimond.

J. BRAHAM, J. DAVY, and W. REEVE: *Thirty Thousand, or, Who's the Richest?*
10 December. Covent Garden
Text by T. J. Dibdin.

1805 J. BRAHAM and W. REEVE: *Out of Place, or, The Lake of Lausanne*
28 February. Covent Garden
Text by Frederic Reynolds. Two acts.

J. HOOK: *The Soldier's Return, or, What can Beauty do?*
23 April. Drury Lane
Text by Theodore Edward Hook. Two acts

M. KELLY: *Youth, Love, and Folly*
24 May. Drury Lane
'A musical entertainment' (Kelly). Text by W. Dimond.

1806 DOMENICO CORRI: *The Travellers, or, Music's Fascination*
22 January. Drury Lane
'An operatic drama'. Text by Andrew Cherry. Five acts—the first in Pekin, the second in Constantinople, the third in Naples, the fourth in Caserta, and the fifth in Portsmouth.

C. DIBDIN: *The Broken Gold*
8 February. Drury Lane
Text by the composer.

W. REEVE: *The White Plume, or, The Border Chieftains*
10 April. Covent Garden
Text by T. J. Dibdin.

J. DAVY: *Spanish Dollars! or, The Priest of the Parish*
9 May. Covent Garden
'An operatic sketch'. Text by Andrew Cherry. One act.

J. HOOK: *Catch him who can!*
12 June. Theatre Royal, Haymarket
Text by T. E. Hook.

M. KELLY: *Adrian and Orrila, or, A Mother's Vengeance*
15 November. Covent Garden
'An operatic play' (Kelly). Text by W. Dimond.

1807 J. BRAHAM, and M. P. KING: *False Alarms, or, My Cousin*
12 January. Drury Lane
Comic opera. Text by James Kenney. Three acts.

M. KELLY: *The Young Hussar, or, Love and Mercy*
12 March. Drury Lane
'Operatic piece'. Text by W. Dimond. Two acts.

M. KELLY: *The Wood Daemon, or, 'The Clock has Struck'*
1 April. Drury Lane.
'Romantic drama' (Kelly). Text by M. G. Lewis.
For a subsequent version, see *One O'Clock!* (1811).

W. SHIELD: *Two Faces under a Hood*
17 November. Covent Garden
Text by T. J. Dibdin.

1808 **W. REEVE and J. BRAHAM**:[1] *Kais, or, Love in the Deserts*
11 February. Drury Lane
Opera. Text by Isaac Brandon. Four acts.

M. KELLY: *The Jew of Mogadore*
3 May. Drury Lane
'Comic opera'. Text by Richard Cumberland. Three acts.

J. HOOK: *The Siege of St Quintin, or, Spanish Heroism*
10 November.[2] Drury Lane
Text by T. E. Hook.

J. MAZZINGHI and HENRY BISHOP: *The Exile, or, The Deserts of Siberia*
10 November. King's, Haymarket
Text by F. Reynolds. Three acts. Presented by the Covent Garden Company.

1809 **H. BISHOP**: *The Circassian Bride*
23 February. Drury Lane
Opera. Text by C. Ward. Three acts.

H. BISHOP: *The Vintagers*
1 August. Theatre Royal, Haymarket
'A musical romance'. Text by Edmund John Eyre. Two acts.

J. HOOK: *Safe and Sound*
28 August. London, Lyceum
Comic opera. Text by T. E. Hook. Three acts. Presented by the Drury Lane Company.

1810 **J. MAZZINGHI**: *The Free Knights, or, The Edict of Charlemagne*
8 February. Covent Garden
Text by F. Reynolds.

(1) According to W. T. Parke (*Musical Memoirs*, 1830) the music was by Henry Bishop.
(2) According to W. T. Parke (*op. cit.*) the date was 26 September.

H. BISHOP: *The Maniac, or, Swiss Banditti*
13 March. London, Lyceum
Text by S. J. Arnold. Three acts. Presented by the Drury Lane Company.

M. P. KING: *Oh! this Love! or, The Masqueraders*
12 June. London, Lyceum
Comic opera. Text by J. Kenney. Presented by the Drury Lane Company.

CHARLES HORN and W. REEVE: *Tricks upon Travellers*
9 July. London, Lyceum
Comic opera. Text by Sir James Bland Burges. Presented by the Drury Lane Company.

M. P. KING: *Plots! or, The North Tower*
3 September. London, Lyceum
Text by S. J. Arnold. Presented by the Drury Lane Company.

M. KELLY: *Gustavus Vasa*
29 November. Covent Garden
'Musical drama' (Kelly). Text by W. Dimond.

1811 M. KELLY: *The Peasant Boy*
31 January. London, Lyceum
'Musical drama' (Kelly). Text by W. Dimond. Presented by the Drury Lane Company.

H. BISHOP: *The Knight of Snowdoun*
5 February. Covent Garden
Text by Thomas Morton, after Scott's *The Lady of the Lake*. Three acts.

M. P. KING and J. BRAHAM: *The Americans*
27 April. London, Lyceum
Comic opera. Text by S. J. Arnold. Presented by the Drury Lane Company.

M. KELLY: *The Royal Oak*
10 June. Theatre Royal, Haymarket
Musical 'drama' (Kelly). Text by W. Dimond.

C. DIBDIN: *The Round Robin*
21 June. Theatre Royal, Haymarket
Charles Dibdin's last piece for the stage. Text by the composer.

M. KELLY and M. P. KING: *One O'Clock! or, The Knight and the Wood Daemon*
1 August. London, Lyceum
This was a new version of *The Wood Daemon* (1807). According to the *Reminiscences of Michael Kelly*, M. G. Lewis, the librettist, 'only made use of the subject—several new characters were introduced.' Presented by the Drury Lane Company.

T. WELSH: *Kamtchatka, or, The Slave's Tribute*
16 October. Covent Garden
'Musical drama'. Text adapted from A. F. F. von Kotzebue by Charles
Kemble. The overture was composed by Ware.

**H. CONDELL, W. REEVE, J. WELSH, and J.
WHITAKER:** *Up to Town*
6 November. Covent Garden
'Opera' (T. J. Dibdin). Text by T. J. Dibdin.

1812 **H. BISHOP:** *The Virgin of the Sun*
31 January. Covent Garden
Text by F. Reynolds, after Kotzebue.

C. E. HORN, and J. BRAHAM: *The Devil's Bridge, or,
The Piedmontese Alps*
6 May. London, Lyceum
Text by S. J. Arnold. Presented by the Drury Lane Company.

SIR JOHN STEVENSON: *The Spanish Patriots a
Thousand Years Ago*
22 September. London, Lyceum
Text by H. B. Code. Presented by the Drury Lane Company.

H. BISHOP: *The Aethiop, or, The Child of the Desert*
6 October. Covent Garden
Text by W. Dimond.
   It appears that this was adapted by T. J. Dibdin and produced at
Covent Garden early in 1813 under the title of *Haroun Alraschid*.

1813 **H. CONDELL and W. WARE:** *Aladdin, or, The
Wonderful Lamp*
19 April. Covent Garden
Text by Charles Farley.
   Farley was responsible for many of the annual pantomimes at Covent
Garden. W. T. Parke (in his *Musical Memoirs*, 1830) called this musical
piece 'a superb Asiatic spectacle' and thought the music 'possessed
considerable merit'.

H. BISHOP: *The Miller and his Men*
21 October. Covent Garden
'Melodramatic piece' (Parke). Text by Isaac Pocock. Two acts.

M. KELLY: *Illusion, or, The Trances of Nourjahad*
25 November. Drury Lane
'Musical piece' (Kelly). Text by S. J. Arnold. Three acts. Described by
T. J. Dibdin in his *Autobiography* (1837) as 'a grand oriental spectacle'.
   See *Nourjahad* (1834).

H. BISHOP: *'For England, Ho!'*
15 December. Covent Garden
'Melodramatic piece' (Parke). Text by Isaac Pocock. Two acts.

1814 J. BRAHAM, and C. E. HORN: *Narensky, or, The Road to Yaroslaf*
11 January. Drury Lane
Comic opera. Text by Charles Armitage Brown.

J. ADDISON, H. BISHOP, H. CONDELL, J. DAVY, W. REEVE, T. WELSH: *The Farmer's Wife*
1 February. Covent Garden
Comic opera. Text by Charles Dibdin the younger. 'It was got up with such expedition as to prove that "many hands make light work".' (*Musical Memoirs* by W. T. Parke, 1830.)

T. COOKE: *Frederick the Great, or, The Heart of a Soldier*
4 August. London, Lyceum
Operetta. Text by S. J. Arnold.

1815 H. BISHOP and W. REEVE: *Brother and Sister*
1 February. Covent Garden
Comic opera. Text by W. Dimond; lyrics by Charles Dibdin the younger. Two acts.

M. KELLY: *The Unknown Guest*
29 March. Drury Lane
'Opera' (Kelly). Text by S. J. Arnold.

T. COOKE: *The King's Proxy, or, Judge for Yourself*
19 August. London, Lyceum
Comic opera. Text by S. J. Arnold.

J. WHITAKER: *My Spouse and I*
7 December. Drury Lane
Text by Charles Dibdin the younger.

1816 H. BISHOP: *A Midsummer Night's Dream*
17 January. Covent Garden
Text by F. Reynolds, after the play by Shakespeare. The music was 'composed and arranged' by Bishop.

T. ATTWOOD, H. BISHOP, and J. WHITAKER: *Guy Mannering, or, The Gipsey's Prophecy*
12 March. Covent Garden
Text by Daniel Terry after the novel by Sir Walter Scott. Written by Terry in collaboration with Scott. Three acts.

H. BISHOP: *Who wants a Wife? or, The Law of the Land*
16 April. Covent Garden
Operatic farce. Text by the composer.

J. ADDISON: *Free and Easy*
16 September. English Opera House[1]
Text by S. J. Arnold.

(1) The former Lyceum Theatre had been reopened on 15 June 1816 under this title after almost complete rebuilding.

H. BISHOP: *The Slave*
12 *November*. Covent Garden
Text by T. Morton. Three acts.

1817   H. BISHOP: *The Humorous Lieutenant, or, Alexander's Successors*
18 *January*. Covent Garden
Text by F. Reynolds.

T. COOKE: *The Innkeeper's Daughter*
7 *April*. Drury Lane
Text by George Soane.

M. KELLY: *The Conquest of Taranto, or, St Clara's Eve*
15 *April*. Covent Garden
Text by W. Dimond.

C. E. HORN: *The Persian Hunters, or, The Rose of Gurgistan*
13 *August*. English Opera House
Text by T. Noble.

1818   M. KELLY: *The Bride of Abydos*
5 *February*. Drury Lane
Text by W. Dimond, after the poem by Lord Byron.

J. BRAHAM and H. BISHOP: *Zuma, or, The Tree of Health*
21 *February*. Covent Garden
Text by T. J. Dibdin.

J. DAVY: *Rob Roy Macgregor, or, Auld Lang Syne!*
12 *March*. Covent Garden
Text by I. Pocock, after the novel by Sir Walter Scott. This version includes songs by Burns and Wordsworth. For the greater part of the music, Davy drew upon popular Scottish airs.

1819   M. KELLY: *Abudah, or, The Talisman of Oromanes*
13 *April*. Drury Lane
Text by James Robinson Planché.

H. BISHOP: *The Heart of Mid-Lothian*
17 *April*. Covent Garden
Text by D. Terry, after the novel by Sir Walter Scott.

H. BISHOP: *The Comedy of Errors*
11 *December*. Covent Garden
Text by F. Reynolds, after the play by Shakespeare.

1820   H. BISHOP and T. COOKE: *The Antiquary*
25 *January*. Covent Garden
Text by I. Pocock and D. Terry, after the novel by Sir Walter Scott.

JOHN PARRY: *Ivanhoe, or, The Knight Templar*
2 March. Covent Garden
Text by Samuel Beazley the younger, after the novel by Sir Walter Scott.

M. KELLY: *The Lady and the Devil*
3 May. Drury Lane
Text by W. Dimond.

H. BISHOP: *The Battle of Bothwell Brigg*
22 May. Covent Garden
Text by Charles Farley, after *Old Mortality* by Sir Walter Scott.

J. BRAHAM, J. ATTWOOD, T. COOKE, and W. REEVE: *David Rizzio*
17 June. Drury Lane
Text by Colonel Ralph Hamilton; songs by Charles Dibdin the younger.
Three acts.

H. BISHOP: *Twelfth Night*
8 November. Covent Garden
Text by F. Reynolds, after the play by Shakespeare. According to Parke's
Musical Memoirs (op. cit.), some of the music was selected 'from
Ravenscroft, Winter, Sir John Stevenson, &c. by Bishop'.

1821   **H. BISHOP and W. WARE:** *Don John, or, The Two Violettas*
20 February. Covent Garden
Text by F. Reynolds, after *The Chances* by Beaumont and Fletcher as
altered by Buckingham.

H. BISHOP: *The Tempest*
15 May. Covent Garden
Text by F. Reynolds, after the play by Shakespeare.

C. E. HORN: *Dirce, or, The Fatal Urn**
2 June. Drury Lane
Text adapted from Metastasio's *Demofoonte*. Three acts.

1822   **H. BISHOP, W. WARE, and WATSON:** *Montrose, or, The Children of the Mist*
14 February. Covent Garden
Text by F. Reynolds, after Sir Walter Scott's *Tales of my Landlord*.

J. WHITAKER, G. PERRY, and T. COOKE: *The Veteran Soldier, or, The Farmer's Sons*
23 February. Drury Lane
Text by Edward P. Knight. Three acts.

H. BISHOP: *The Law of Java*
11 May. Covent Garden
Text by G. Colman the younger. Three acts.

G. PERRY: *Morning, Noon and Night, or, The Romance of a Day*
9 September. Theatre Royal, Haymarket
Text by T. J. Dibdin.

H. BISHOP: *Maid Marian, or, The Huntress of Arlingford*
3 December. Covent Garden
Text by J. R. Planché, after the novel by T. L. Peacock. Three acts.

1823   **C. E. HORN**: *Philandering, or, The Rose Queen*
13 January. Drury Lane
Text by Samuel Beazley the younger. Three acts.

H. BISHOP: *Clari, or, The Maid of Milan*
8 May. Covent Garden
Text by John Howard Payne. Three acts.

J. WHITAKER, ISAAC NATHAN, T. COOKE, and G. PERRY: *Sweethearts and Wives*
7 July. Theatre Royal, Haymarket
Comic opera. Text by J. Kenney.

H. BISHOP: *Cortez, or, The Conquest of Mexico*
5 November. Covent Garden
Text by J. R. Planché. Three acts.

1824   **H. BISHOP**: *Native Land, or, The Return from Slavery*
10 February. Covent Garden
Text by W. Dimond. Three acts. According to Parke (*op. cit.*), 'the music was composed and selected from Rossini, by Bishop'.

H. BISHOP: *The Merry Wives of Windsor*
20 February. Drury Lane
Text by F. Reynolds, after the play by Shakespeare.

W. REEVE: *The Frozen Lake*
3 September. English Opera House
Text by J. R. Planché, after Scribe's *La neige, ou, le nouvel Eginard*.

1825   **H. BISHOP**: *The Fall of Algiers*
19 January. Drury Lane
Text by C. E. Walker. (It is thought that J. H. Payne may also have been involved.) Three acts.

H. BISHOP: *Masaniello, the Fisherman of Naples*
17 February. Drury Lane
Text by George Soane. Five acts.

SIR JOHN STEVENSON: *The Cavern, or, The Outlaws*
22 April. Dublin, Theatre Royal, Hawkins Street
Text by Sarah Isdell (Lady Morgan).

C. E. HORN: *The Wedding Present*
28 October. Drury Lane
Text by J. Kenney. Three acts.

1826   T. COOKE: *Malvina*
28 January. Drury Lane
'National ballad opera'. Text by George Macfarren. Three acts.

J. WHITAKER: *The Apprentice's Opera, or, The Fate of the Fancy Lad*
27 March. London, Surrey
Text by Charles Dibdin the younger.

[CARL MARIA VON WEBER: *Oberon, or, The Elf King's Oath*
12 April. Covent Garden
Text by J. R. Planché, after the poem of C. M. Wieland. Three acts.]

H. BISHOP: *Aladdin*
29 April. Drury Lane
'A fairy opera'. Text by G. Soane. Three acts.

J. WHITAKER: *The Rake's Progress*
10 July. London, Surrey
Text by Charles Dibdin the younger.

JOHN BARNETT: *Before Breakfast*
31 August. English Opera House
Operatic farce. Text by R. B. Peake.

C. E. HORN: *Peveril of the Peak*
21 October. Covent Garden
Text by I. Pocock, after the novel by Sir Walter Scott.

1827   H. BISHOP: *Englishmen in India*
27 January. Drury Lane
Comic opera. Text by W. Dimond.

I. NATHAN: *The Illustrious Stranger, or, Married and Buried*
1 October. Drury Lane
Operatic farce. Text by J. Kenney (written in collaboration with J. Millengen).

S. STORACE: *Isidore de Merida, or, The Devil's Creek*
29 November. Drury Lane
A revival of *The Pirates* (1792) with additional music by Braham, Cooke, Mercadante, and Balducci.

1828   H. BISHOP: *Edward the Black Prince*
28 January. Drury Lane
Text by F. Reynolds, after the play by William Shirley. The musical score and lyrics are in The British Library (Add. MS. 27722).

J. BRAHAM, T. COOKE, and OTHERS: *The Taming of the Shrew*
14 May. Drury Lane
Operatic farce, after the play by Shakespeare. This pasticcio score including borrowings from Rossini, Mercadante, and Sir John Stevenson.

A. LEE: *Auld Robin Grey*
17 May. London, Surrey
Operetta. Text by G. Macfarren.
   An alteration of this operetta with music by T. Mackinlay and the text adapted by E. Fitzball was produced at the Surrey Theatre on 19 April 1858.

1829 **J. BARNETT:** *Monsieur Mallet, or, My Daughter's Letter*
22 January. London, Adelphi
Operetta. Text by Thomas Moncrieff. The manuscript full score is in the Boston Public Library, Massachusetts.

1830 **J. BARNETT:** *Robert the Devil*
2 February. Covent Garden
Musical drama. The manuscript full score is in the Boston Public Library, Mass.

MICHAEL WILLIAM BALFE: *I Rivali di se stessi**
Spring. Palermo, Teatro Carolino
Italian text by A. Alcazar, after the French farce by Le Brun entitled *Les Rivaux d'eux-mêmes*. Two acts.

LORD BURGHERSH: *Catherine, or, The Austrian Captive*
6 November. King's, Haymarket
'A musical drama'. Text based on Cobb's libretto for *The Siege of Belgrade* (1791). Three acts. 'Performed experimentally by the pupils of the Royal Academy of Music'.
   Lord Burghersh also composed four serious operas—*Bajazette* (1821), *L'Eroe di Lancastro* (1826), *Fedra* (1828), *Il Torneo* (1829)—and an operetta and an opera buffa entitled *Il Ratto di Proserpina* and *Lo Scompiglio* (1836) respectively. Most of these were given private performances in Florence where he served for several years as English envoy extraordinary and minister plenipotentiary. For a public performance of *Il Torneo*, see the entry in this Register under 1838. The vocal score of *Fedra* was published about 1848 in Berlin, where he was then serving as British Ambassador.

1831 **H. BISHOP:** *The Romance of a Day*
3 February. Covent Garden
Text by J. R. Planché.

M. W. BALFE: *Un Avvertmento ai Gelosi**
Spring. Pavia, Teatro Fraschini
'Farsa giocosa'. Italian text by G. Foppa. One act.

GEORGE H. RODWELL: *The Skeleton Lover*
16 July. London, Adelphi
Musical drama. This was presented by the English Opera House Company at the Adelphi, the Lyceum having been burnt down in 1830.

[FERDINAND RIES: *The Sorceress*
4 August. London, Adelphi
Text by Edward Fitzball, after the story by C. F. van der Velde. Two acts. Presented by the English Opera House Company.
   Die Räuberbraut by Ries (first produced at Frankfurt on 15 October 1828) had been a great success when played in London in English. Rival versions were given—at the English Opera House (15 July 1829) and Covent Garden (22 October 1829). Ries was then invited to write an opera for the English stage; but *The Sorceress* was a failure.]

1832 J. BARNETT: *Win Her and Wear Her*
18 December. Drury Lane
Comic opera. Adapted from Mrs Centlivre's comedy, *A Bold Stroke for a Wife*. Three acts. The manuscript full score is in the Boston Public Library, Mass.

1833 M. W. BALFE: *Enrico Quarto al Passo della Marna**
19 February. Milan, Teatro Carcano
The author of the Italian libretto is unknown. One act.

1834 EDWARD JAMES LODER: *Nourjahad*
21 July. English Opera House
Text by S. J. Arnold, originally set to music by M. Kelly. (See *Illusion*, 1813.) Three acts.
   The Lyceum Theatre, then known as the English Opera House, had been rebuilt in 1833/4.

A. LEE: *The Dragon*
4 August. English Opera House
Comic opera. Text by John Maddison Morton.

J. BARNETT: *The Mountain Sylph**
25 August. English Opera House
Text by Thomas James Thackeray. Two acts. The manuscript full score is in the Boston Public Library, Mass.

JOHN THOMSON: *Hermann, or, The Broken Spear*
27 October. English Opera House
Librettist unknown.

GEORGE ALEXANDER MACFARREN: *Genevieve, The Maid of Switzerland*
3 November. English Opera House
Operetta. Text by Mrs Cornwell Baron-Wilson.
   G. A. Macfarren was the son of G. Macfarren, the librettist; and in some reminiscences of early family history that he sketched, and which are quoted in *George Alexander Macfarren* by Henry C. Banister (London, G. Bell & Sons, 1891), there is a reference to this operetta, which

might lead one to think it had been played at an earlier date (about 1831?) at the Queen's Theatre, Tottenham Street.

J. TEMPLETON: *The Red Mask, or, The Council of Three*
15 November. Drury Lane
Text by J. R. Planché, after Fenimore Cooper.

G. H. RODWELL: *The Lord of the Isles, or, The Gathering of the Clans*
20 November. London, Surrey
Text by E. Fitzball, after the poem by Sir Walter Scott.

1835   **PACKER:** *Sadak and Kalasrade, or, The Waters of Oblivion*
20 April. English Opera House
Romantic opera. Text by Mary Russell Mitford. Two acts.
   A serio-comic pantomime with the same title was written by T. J. Dibdin and produced at Sadler's Wells in 1796.

J. THOMSON: *The Shadow on the Wall*
24 April. English Opera House
Musical drama. Text by T. J. Serle.

G. H. RODWELL: *The Spirit of the Bell*
8 June. English Opera House
Comic opera. Text by J. Kenney.

E. J. LODER: *The Covenanters*
10 August. English Opera House
Ballad opera. Text by T. J. Dibdin.

E. J. LODER: *The Dice of Death*
14 September. English Opera House
Musical drama. Text by J. Oxenford.

G. H. RODWELL: *Paul Clifford*
28 October. Covent Garden
Musical drama. Text by E. Fitzball, after the novel by Bulwer Lytton. Three acts.

M. W. BALFE: *The Siege of Rochelle*
29 October. Drury Lane
Text by E. Fitzball. Two acts. The autograph manuscript full score is in the British Library (Add. MS. 29, 325–6).

MRS G. A. à BECKETT: *Agnes Sorel*
14 December. London, St James's
Text by Gilbert Abbott à Beckett.

1836   **M. W. BALFE:** *The Maid of Artois*
26 May. Drury Lane
Text by Alfred Bunn. Three acts. The autograph manuscript full score is in the British Library (Add. MS. 29, 327–8).

[JULIUS BENEDICT: *Un Anno ed un Giorno**
19 October. Naples, Fondo
Italian text by the Marchese D. Andreotti. One act. The last opera
Benedict wrote in Italy before settling in London, where it was played (in
Italian also) at the English Opera House on 31 January 1837.

Benedict had previously produced in Italy *Giacinta ed Ernesto* (Naples
1829) and *I Portoghesi in Goa* (Naples 1830).]

JOHN PYKE HULLAH: *The Village Coquettes*
6 December. London, St James's
Text by Charles Dickens. Two acts.

1837 [MICHAEL COSTA: *Malek Adel*
14 January. Paris, Théâtre Italien
Italian text by C. Pepoli, after S. Cottin. Three acts. It was also
performed in London at the King's Theatre in the Haymarket on 18 May
1837.

Costa had previously written *Malvina* for production at Naples in 1829.]

J. BARNETT: *Fair Rosamond*
28 February. Drury Lane
Text by C. Z. Barnett. Four acts. The manuscript full score is in the
Boston Public Library, Mass.

M. W. BALFE: *Catherine Gray**
27 May. Drury Lane
Text by George Linley. Three acts. The autograph manuscript full score is
in the British Library (Add. MS. 29, 329–30).

ALEXANDER LEE: *The Afrancesado, or, Secrecy and
Truth*
19 October. Covent Garden
Musical drama. Text by T. J. Serle.

J. P. HULLAH: *The Barbers of Bassora*
11 November. Covent Garden
Operatic farce. Text by John Maddison Morton. Two acts. The manuscript full score is in the Boston Public Library, Mass.

M. W. BALFE: *Joan of Arc*
30 November. Drury Lane
Text by E. Fitzball. Three acts. The autograph manuscript full score is in
the British Library (Add. MS. 29, 331–2).

WILLIAM MICHAEL ROOKE: *Amilie, or, The Love Test*
2 December. Covent Garden
Text by John Thomas Haines. Three acts. (This opera had been composed twenty years earlier.)

1838 J. BENEDICT: *The Gipsy's Warning*
19 April. Drury Lane
Text by G. Linley and R. B. Peake. Two acts. Benedict's first English
opera.

J. P. HULLAH: *The Outpost*
17 May. Covent Garden
Operetta. Librettist unknown.

M. W. BALFE: *Diadesté, or, The Veiled Lady*
17 May. Drury Lane
Opera buffa. Text by E. Fitzball. Two acts. The autograph manuscript
full score is in the British Library (Add. MS. 29, 333).

M. W. BALFE: *Falstaff**
19 July. Her Majesty's[1]
Italian text by S. M. Maggioni. Two acts. The autograph manuscript full
score is in the British Library (Add. MS. 29, 334).

LORD BURGHERSH: *Il Torneo*
20 July. London, St James's
It is likely that this opera had received a private performance in Florence
about 1829.

G. A. MACFARREN (the younger): *The Devil's Opera*
13 August. English Opera House
Text by G. Macfarren (the elder). Two acts.

E. J. LODER: *The Foresters, or, Twenty-five Years Since*
19 October. Covent Garden
Text by T. J. Serle.

E. J. LODER: *Francis I*
6 November. Drury Lane
Text by McKinlan.

1839   J. BARNETT: *Farinelli*
8 February. Drury Lane
Serio-comic opera. Text by C. Z. Barnett. Two acts. The manuscript full
score is in the Boston Public Library, Mass.

M. W. ROOKE: *Henrique, or, The Love Pilgrim*
2 May. Covent Garden
Text by J. T. Haines. Three acts.

1840   CORNELIUS BRYAN: *Lundy in the Olden Time*
27 March. Bristol, Theatre Royal
Text by Miss Bryan.

F. ROMER: *Fridolin*
26 November. London, Prince's (St James's)
Burletta. Text by Mark Lemon.

1841   M. W. BALFE: *Keolanthe, or, The Unearthly Bride*
9 March. English Opera House
Text by E. Fitzball. Two acts.

(1) Between 1837 and 1901 the King's Theatre in the Haymarket was styled Her
Majesty's Theatre.

Balfe made a revised three-act version, with seven additional numbers, for production in Vienna in 1857.

E. J. LODER: *The Deer Stalker, or, The Outlaw's Daughter*
12 April. English Opera House.
Text by Mark Lemon.

HARROWAY: *Arcadia, or, The Shepherd and the Shepherdess*
19 April. London, Grecian
Operetta. Text by Edward Leman Blanchard.

SAMUEL LOVER: *Il Paddy Whack in Italia*
22 April. English Opera House
Opera buffa. Text by the composer.

1842 **G. H. RODWELL:** *The Students of Bonn*
21 March. Drury Lane
Operetta. Text by the composer.

CHARLES NAGEL: *The Mock Catalani in Little Puddleton*
4 May. Sydney, Victoria Theatre (New South Wales)
Musical burletta. Text by the composer. 'A piece written in the Colony.'

1843 **JOHN LIPTROTT HATTON:** *The Queen of the Thames, or, The Anglers*
25 February. Drury Lane
Operetta. Text by E. Fitzball.

M. W. BALFE: *Le Puits d'Amour*
20 April. Paris, Opéra Comique
French text by A. E. Scribe and A. de Leuven. Three acts.
The English version, entitled *Geraldine, or, The Lover's Well*, was produced in London at the Princess's Theatre on 14 August 1843 in a translation by G. A. à Beckett.
The autograph manuscript full score is in the British Library (Add. MS. 29, 337–8).

M. W. BALFE: *The Bohemian Girl*
27 November. Drury Lane
Text by Alfred Bunn, after *La Gipsy*, a ballet-pantomime by J. H. Vernoy de Saint-Georges. Three acts.
An Italian version with recitatives, entitled *La Zingara*, was given at Her Majesty's on 6 February 1858.
Two autograph manuscript full scores are in the British Library: one with English text (Add. MS. 29, 335), the other with French text (Add. MS. 29, 336).

1844 **J. L. HATTON:** *Pasqual Bruno*
2 March. Vienna, Kärntnertortheater
Text by E. Fitzball. Three acts. German translation by J. von Seyfried. Never produced in England.

J. BENEDICT: *The Brides of Venice*
22 April. Drury Lane
Text by A. Bunn and the composer. Two acts.

ANON: *The Currency Lass*
27 May. Sydney, N.S.W., Victoria Theatre
'Original musical piece'. Text by Edward Geoghegan. This piece contained fourteen songs set to popular airs of the day.

M. COSTA: *Don Carlos**
20 June. Her Majesty's
Italian text by L. Tarantini. Three acts.

M. W. BALFE: *Les Quatre Fils Aymon*
15 July. Paris, Opéra Comique
French text by A. de Leuven and L. L. Brunswick. Three acts.

The English version, entitled *The Castle of Aymon, or, The Four Brothers*, was produced in London at the Princess's Theatre on 20 November 1844 in a translation by G. A. à Beckett.

An Italian version with recitative, in a translation by Maggioni, entitled *I Quattro Fratelli*, was given at Her Majesty's on 11 August 1851.

The autograph manuscript full score is in the British Library (Add. MS. 29, 339–40).

M. W. BALFE: *The Daughter of St Mark**
27 November. Drury Lane
Text by A. Bunn, after J. H. Vernoy de Saint-Georges's libretto for Halévy's La Reine de *Chypre* (1841). Three acts. The autograph manuscript full score is in the British Library (Add. MS. 29, 341–3).

1845   [FELIX MENDELSSOHN: *Antigone*
2 January. Covent Garden
Text by B. Bartholomew, adapted from the German.

This operatic arrangement of Mendelssohn's music for the play of Sophocles was put on in London for a single performance. It does not appear to have been successful. (See *The Annals of Covent Garden Theatre* by Henry Saxe Wyndham. London, Chatto & Windus, 1906.)]

M. W. BALFE: *The Enchantress*
14 May. Drury Lane
Text by A. Bunn, after J. H. Vernoy de Saint-Georges. Three acts. The autograph manuscript full score is in the British Library (Add. MS. 29, 344–5).

HENRY FORBES: *The Fairy Oak*
18 October. Drury Lane
Text by H. C. Coape. Three acts.

WILLIAM VINCENT WALLACE: *Maritana*
15 November. Drury Lane
Text by E. Fitzball, after *Don César de Bazan* by d'Ennery and Pinel Dumanoir. Three acts.

M. W. BALFE: *L'Etoile de Séville**
17 December. Paris, Opéra
Text by H. Lucas. Three acts. Never produced in England.

1846 G. A. MACFARREN (the younger): *An Adventure of Don Quixote*
3 February. Drury Lane
Text by G. Macfarren (the elder). Two acts.

J. BENEDICT: *The Crusaders*
26 February. Drury Lane
Text by A. Bunn. Three acts.

I. NATHAN: *Triboulet, the King's Jester*
21 April. Sydney, Victoria Theatre
Author unknown.

E. J. LODER: *The Night Dancers*
28 October. London, Princess's
Grand romantic opera. Text by G. Soane. Two acts. The manuscript full score is in the Library of Congress, Washington D.C.

LAVENU: *Loretta, a Tale of Seville*
9 November. Drury Lane
Text by A. Bunn. Three acts.

M. W. BALFE: *The Bondman*
11 December. Drury Lane
Text by A. Bunn, after Mélesville's *Le Chevalier de Saint-George.* Three acts. The autograph manuscript full score is in the British Library (Add. MS. 29, 346–7).

G. H. RODWELL: *The Seven Maids of Munich, or, The Ghost's Tower*
19 December. London, Princess's
Text by the composer.

1847 HENRY DEVAL: *The Rival Clans*
27 January. Newcastle upon Tyne, Theatre Royal
Ballad opera. Text by the composer.

W. V. WALLACE: *Matilda of Hungary*
22 February. Drury Lane
Text by A. Bunn. Three acts.

I. NATHAN: *Don John of Austria*
3 May. Sydney, Victoria Theatre
Text by J. L. Montefiore.
  In the Sydney press this was referred to as 'the first opera written, composed, and submitted to an Australian theatre'—but see *The Mock Catalani in Little Puddleton* (1842), *The Currency Lass* (1844), and *Triboulet, the King's Jester* (1846). The libretto of *Don John of Austria* and a piano reduction of the score are extant.

J. H. TULLY: *The Forest Maiden and the Moorish Page*
31 May. London, Surrey
Text by E. Fitzball.

M. W. BALFE: *The Maid of Honour*
20 December. Drury Lane
Text by E. Fitzball. Three acts. The autograph manuscript full score is in
the British Library (Add. MS. 29, 348–9).

1848 H. H. PIERSON: *Leila*
22 February. Hamburg
German text by C. Leonhardt-Lyser. Three acts.
   In 1845 H. H. Pearson, who had been Professor of Music at Edinburgh
University, resigned his post and retired to Germany, where he altered
the spelling of his name and composed four operas, of which *Leila* was the
first, but none of which was ever performed in Great Britain.

J. H. TULLY: *Jeannette and Jeannot*
14 September. Brighton, Theatre Royal
Text by H. Horncastle.

E. J. LODER: *Robin Goodfellow, or, The Frolics of Puck*
6 December. London, Princess's
Ballad Opera. Text by the composer.

H. R. LAURENT: *Quentin Durward*
6 December. Covent Garden
Text by E. Fitzball.

1849 G. A. MACFARREN: *King Charles II*
27 October. London, Princess's
Text by M. Desmond Ryan. Two acts.

1850 G. A. MACFARREN: *The Sleeper Awakened*
15 November. Her Majesty's

1851 E. F. FITZWILLIAM: *The Queen of a Day*
13 August. Theatre Royal, Haymarket
Librettist unknown.

1852 M. W. BALFE: *The Sicilian Bride*
6 March. Drury Lane
Text by A. Bunn. Four acts. The autograph manuscript full score is in the
British Library (Add. MS. 29, 350–1).

M. W. BALFE: *The Devil's in it.*
26 July. London, Surrey
Text by A. Bunn. Prologue and three acts.
   Produced in New York (17 December 1852) as *The Basket Maker's
Wife*. Revived in London at the Gaiety Theatre (14 June 1871) as *Letty,
the Basket Maker* (text rewritten by John Palgrave Simpson). See also *The
Devil to Pay* (1731).

[LOUIS JULLIEN: *Pietro il Grande*
17 August. Covent Garden
Italian text by S. M. Maggioni. Three acts.]

1853 E. F. FITZWILLIAM: *Love's Alarms*
17 November. Theatre Royal, Haymarket
Text by the composer.

1854 M. W. BALFE: *Pittore e Duca**
21 November. Trieste, Teatro Comunale
Italian text by F. M. Piave. Prologue and three acts.
    The date of this first performance has often been given wrongly in the past. Balfe led the confusion by giving 1852 as the year, in a list of his operas that he drew up towards the end of his life. Balfe's biographer, William Alexander Barrett, gave September 1856 as the date.
    See also *Moro* (1882).

1855 FOURNESS ROLFE: *The Minstrel's Return, or, The Sultan's Jubilee*
22 March. Newcastle upon Tyne, Theatre Royal
Musical interlude. Text by the composer.

HENRY SMART: *Berta, or, The Gnome of the Hartsberg*
29 May. Theatre Royal, Haymarket
Operetta. Text by Hawley Smart.

E. J. LODER: *Raymond and Agnes*
14 August. Manchester, Theatre Royal
Romantic opera. Text by E. Fitzball. Three acts. The manuscript full score is in the Library of Congress, Washington D.C.

1857 M. W. BALFE: *The Rose of Castille*
29 October. London, Lyceum
Text by A. G. Harris and E. Falconer. Three acts. The autograph manuscript full score is in the British Library (Add. MS. 29, 352–3).

1858 M. W. BALFE: *Satanella, or, The Power of Love*
20 December. Covent Garden
Text by A. G. Harris and E. Falconer. Four acts. The autograph manuscript full score is in the British Library (Add. MS. 29, 354–5).

1859 MEYER LUTZ: *Zaida, or, The Pearl of Granada*
14 February. Liverpool, Amphitheatre
Text by Oliver Summers, from the German of Dr. Franks.

E. J. LODER: *Never Judge by Appearances*
7 July. London, Adelphi
Operetta. Text by H. Drayton.

A. MELLON: *Victorine*
19 December. Covent Garden
Text by E. Falconer. Three acts.

1860 FREDERIC H. COWEN: *Garibaldi, or, The Rival Patriots*
'Drawing Room Operetta'. Text by 'Rosalind'. Two acts. This operetta
was composed by Cowen at the age of eight and performed privately by
his relatives and friends in London.

W. V. WALLACE: *Lurline*
23 February. Covent Garden
Text by E. Fitzball. Three acts. According to Richard Northcott the
manuscript score is in the Library of the Conservatoire Royal de
Musique, Brussels.

G. A. MACFARREN: *Robin Hood*
11 October. Her Majesty's
Text by Oxenford. Three acts.

M. W. BALFE: *Bianca, the Bravo's Bride*
6 December. Covent Garden
Text by J. P. Simpson, after M. G. Lewis. Four acts. The autograph
manuscript full score is in the British Library (Add. MS. 29, 356–7).

1861 W. V. WALLACE: *The Amber Witch*
28 February. Her Majesty's
Text by H. F. Chorley, after W. Meinhold. Four acts.

WILLIAM HOWARD GLOVER: *Ruy Blas*
24 October. Covent Garden
Text by the composer, after Victor Hugo. Three acts.

FREDERICK CLAY: *Court and Cottage*
11 November. Covent Garden
Operetta. Text by Tom Taylor.

M. W. BALFE: *The Puritan's Daughter*
30 November. Covent Garden
Text by John V. Bridgeman. Three acts. The autograph manuscript full
score is in the British Library (Add. MS. 29, 358–60).

1862 J. BENEDICT: *The Lily of Killarney*
10 February. Covent Garden
Text by J. Oxenford and D. Boucicault. Three acts.

W. V. WALLACE: *Love's Triumph*
3 November. Covent Garden
Text by J. R. Planché. Three acts. The manuscript full score is in the
British Library (Add. MS. 37211–3).

1863 M. W. BALFE: *The Armourer of Nantes*
12 February. Covent Garden
Text by J. V. Bridgeman. Four acts. The autograph manuscript full score
is in the British Library (Add. MS. 29, 363–4).

G. A. MACFARREN: *The Soldier's Legacy, or, The Old Corporal's Story*
10 July. London, Marylebone Theatre
'Opera da camera'. Text by J. Oxenford. Two acts.

There is some doubt about the year of this operetta's first performance. Allardyce Nicoll (*A History of English Drama*) is the authority for the date here given; but Henry C. Banister, in his monograph on Macfarren, specifically states that it followed a year after *Jessy Lea*.

GEORGE LEMAN SAUNDERS: *A Lord for an Hour*
17 July. Sheffield, Theatre Royal
Text by the composer.

W. V. WALLACE: *The Desert Flower*
12 October. Covent Garden
Text by A. G. Harris and T. J. Williams. Three acts.

G. A. MACFARREN: *Jessy Lea*
2 November. London, Royal Gallery of Illustration (Lower Regent Street) 'Opera di camera'. Text by J. Oxenford, after Scribe. Two acts.

M. W. BALFE: *Blanche de Nevers*
21 November. Covent Garden
Text by John Brougham. Four acts.

The year of the first performance of this opera is sometimes erroneously given as 1862.

The autograph manuscript full score is in the British Library (Add. MS. 29, 361–2).

1864 ### G. A. MACFARREN: *She Stoops to Conquer*
10 February. Covent Garden
Text by E. Fitzball. (N.B.—According to the printed libretto, the date of the first performance was 11 February 1864.)

G. A. MACFARREN: *The Soldier's Legacy*
10 July. London, Marylebone Theatre
'Opera di camera'. Text by J. Oxenford.

M. W. BALFE: *The Sleeping Queen*
31 August. London, Royal Gallery of Illustration
Operetta. Text by Henry Brougham Farnie. One act.

This was originally composed for piano and harmonium. An orchestral version was made by Balfe in 1865.

G. A. MACFARREN: *Helvellyn*
3 November. Covent Garden
Text by J. Oxenford. Four acts.

J. L. HATTON: *Rose, or, Love's Ransom*
26 November. Covent Garden
Text by H. Sutherland Edwards.

J. BENEDICT: *The Bride of Song*
3 December. Covent Garden
Operetta. Text by H. B. Farnie. One act.

1865   **F. CLAY:** *Constance*
23 January. Covent Garden
Operetta. Text by Thomas William Robertson.

HENRY LESLIE: *Ida, or, The Guardian Storks*
15 November. Covent Garden
Text by John Palgrave Simpson.

1867   **ARTHUR SULLIVAN:** *Cox and Box, or, The Long Lost Brothers*
11 May. London, Adelphi Theatre
Comic operetta. Text by F. C. Burnand, after J. M. Morton. One act.

THOMAS L. SELBY: *Adela*
17 May. Nottingham, New Theatre Royal
Text by J. R. Brown.

T. A. WALLWORTH: *Kevin's Choice*
2 December. London, St George's Opera House[1]
Operetta. Text by Miss Hazlewood. Two acts.

A. SULLIVAN: *The Contrabandista, or, The Law of the Ladrones*
18 December. London, St George's Opera House.
Comic opera. Text by F. C. Burnand. Two acts.

1869   **L. ELLIOTT:** *No Cards*
29 March. London, Royal Gallery of Illustration
Musical Comedietta. Text by William Schwenk Gilbert. One act.

F. CLAY: *Ages Ago: A Ghost Story*
22 November. London, Royal Gallery of Illustration
Operetta. Text by W. S. Gilbert. One act.

1870   **F. CLAY:** *The Gentleman in Black*
26 May. London, Charing Cross Theatre
Musical comedietta. Text by W. S. Gilbert.

1871   **GERMAN REED:** *A Sensation Novel*
30 January. London, Royal Gallery of Illustration
Operetta. Text by W. S. Gilbert. One act.

M. W. BALFE: *Letty, the Basket-Maker*
14 June. London, Gaiety
A revised version of *The Devil's in it* (1852) with the text rewritten by John Palgrave Simpson.

(1) Sometimes known as St George's Hall. It was situated in Langham Place, Oxford Circus.

A. SULLIVAN: *Thespis, or, The Gods Grown Old*
26 December. London, Gaiety
'An original grotesque opera'. Text by W. S. Gilbert. Two acts. The first fruit of the Gilbert and Sullivan collaboration.

One song ('Little Maid of Arcadee') was published in 1872; and one number was later transferred to the score of *The Pirates of Penzance* (1879). Otherwise the music has been lost.

A performing edition, using other Sullivan music for the remaining numbers, was made by Terence Rees and Garth Morton in 1962; and this version was first performed at the University of London Union on 4 December 1962.

1872 CARL SCHMITT: *Cazille*
8 April. Sydney, N.S.W., Masonic Hall
Text by Richard Hengist Horne. Three acts.

H. H. PIERSON: *Contarini, oder, Die Verschwörung zu Padua*
16 April. Hamburg
German text by M. E. Lindau. Five acts. Written as early as 1853. Revived in Dessau as *Fenice* (1883).

F. CLAY: *Happy Arcadia*
28 October. London, Royal Gallery of Illustration
Operetta. Text by W. S. Gilbert.

1874 M. W. BALFE: *Il Talismano*
11 June. Drury Lane
Original English text (*The Knight of the Leopard*) by A. Matthison, after the novel by Sir Walter Scott. Italian version by G. Zaffira. Three acts.

Balfe's last opera, originally written in 1866, and produced four years after his death.

1875 A. SULLIVAN: *Trial by Jury**
25 March. London, Royalty
'A novel and original cantata'. Text by W. S. Gilbert. One act.

A. SULLIVAN: *The Zoo**
5 June. London, St James's
'Musical folly'. Text by 'B. Rowe' (*i.e.* B. C. Stephenson).

The music was not published in Sullivan's lifetime; but the autograph manuscript full score came up for auction at Sotheby's on 13 June 1966, when it was bought by Terence Rees, who subsequently edited it for publication.

F. PASCAL: *Eyes and No Eyes, or, The Art of Seeing*
5 July. London, St George's Opera House
Comedietta. Text by W. S. Gilbert.

1876 F. CLAY: *Princess Toto*
1 July. Nottingham
Comic opera. Text by W. S. Gilbert.

F. CLAY: *Don Quixote*
25 September. London, Alhambra
Comic opera. Text by Harry Paulton and A. Maltby.

F. H. COWEN: *Pauline*
22 November. London, Lyceum
Text by H. Hersee, after E. Bulwer Lytton's *The Lady of Lyons*.
Presented by the Carl Rosa Opera Company.

1877 [LAURO ROSSI: *Biorn*
17 January. London, Queen's
Text by F. Marshall, after Shakespeare's *Macbeth*. Five acts.]

A. SULLIVAN: *The Sorcerer, or, The Elixir of Love*
17 November. London, Opéra Comique
'An original modern comic opera'. Text by W. S. Gilbert. Two acts.

1878 A. SULLIVAN: *H.M.S. Pinafore, or, The Lass that Loved a Sailor*
25 May. London, Opéra Comique
'An entirely original nautical comic opera'. Text by W. S. Gilbert. Two acts.

JOSEPH PARRY: *Blodwen*
20 June. Swansea, Music Hall
Text by W. Rowlands. Three acts. The first Welsh opera. Vocal score (Welsh text by 'Mynydogg' or Richard Davies) published in 1915.

1879 A. GORING THOMAS: *The Light of the Harem*
7 November. London, Royal Academy of Music
Text by Clifford Harrison, after the poem by Thomas Moore. Three acts.
    Only part of this opera was performed at the R.A.M.

A. SULLIVAN: *The Pirates of Penzance, or, Love and Duty*
30 December. Paignton, Bijou Theatre
'An entirely original comic opera'. Text by W. S. Gilbert. Two acts.
    The Paignton production was a copyright performance. On 31 December 1879 the operetta was produced at the New Fifth Avenue Theatre, New York. In London it was first given at the Opéra Comique on 3 April 1880 with the subtitle altered to *The Slave of Duty*.

1881 CHARLES VILLIERS STANFORD: *Der Verschleierte Profet**
6 February. Hanover
Original English text (*The Veiled Prophet of Khorassan*) by Barclay Squire. German translation by E. Frank. Three acts.
    Revived (with alterations) in an Italian translation by G. A. Mazzucato at Covent Garden on 26 July 1893.

A. SULLIVAN: *Patience, or, Bunthorne's Bride*
23 April. London, Opéra Comique

'An entirely original aesthetic opera'. Text by W. S. Gilbert. Two acts. Transferred to the Savoy Theatre (which it inaugurated) on 10 October 1881.

1882 M. W. BALFE: *Moro, or, The Painter of Antwerp*
28 January. Her Majesty's
An English version of *Pittore e Duca* (1854) made by W. A. Barrett.

A. SULLIVAN: *Iolanthe, or, The Peer and the Peri*
25 November. London, Savoy
            New York, Standard
Comic opera. Text by W. S. Gilbert. Two acts.

1883 A. GORING THOMAS: *Esmeralda**
26 March. Drury Lane
Text by T. J. H. Marzials and A. Randegger, after Victor Hugo's *Notre Dame de Paris*. Four acts. Presented by the Carl Rosa Opera Company.

ALEXANDER CAMPBELL MACKENZIE: *Colomba**
9 April. Drury Lane
'Lyrical drama'. Text by F. Hueffer, after Prosper Mérimée. Four acts. Presented by the Carl Rosa Opera Company.
   A revised version in three acts was made by the composer with the help of Claude Aveling in 1912.

ISIDORE DE LARA: *The Royal Ward*
17 April. London, Gaiety
Comic opera. Text by Henry Hersee.

JOHN FARMER: *Cinderella: A Little Opera for Big Children, or, A Big Opera for Little Children*
December. Harrow
'A fairy opera'. Text by Henry S. Leigh. Four acts.

1884 A. SULLIVAN: *Princess Ida, or, Castle Adamant*
5 January. London, Savoy
'A respectful operatic perversion of Tennyson's *Princess*'. Text by W. S. Gilbert. Three acts.

C. V. STANFORD: *Savonarola**
18 April. Hamburg
Text by G. A. à Beckett. German translation by E. Frank. Prologue and three acts.

C. V. STANFORD: *The Canterbury Pilgrims**
23 April. Drury Lane
Text by G. A. à Beckett. Three acts. Presented by the Carl Rosa Opera Company.

1885 A. SULLIVAN: *The Mikado, or, The Town of Titipu*
14 March. London, Savoy

'An entirely new and original Japanese opera'. Text by W. S. Gilbert. Two acts. The original manuscript score was bequeathed by the composer to the Royal Academy of Music.

A. G. THOMAS: *Nadeshda**
16 April. Drury Lane
'Romantic opera'. Text by Julian Sturgis. Four acts. Presented by the Carl Rosa Opera Company.

1886 ## A. C. MACKENZIE: *The Troubadour**
8 June. Drury Lane
Text by F. Hueffer. Presented by the Carl Rosa Opera Company.

ALFRED CELLIER: *Dorothy*
25 September. London, Gaiety
Operetta. Text by B. C. Stephenson. Three acts.

1887 ## A. SULLIVAN: *Ruddygore,* [1] *or, the Witch's Curse*
22 January. London, Savoy
'An entirely original supernatural opera'. Text by W. S. Gilbert, after *Ages Ago* (1869). Two acts.

FREDERICK CORDER: *Nordisa**
26 January. Liverpool, Royal Court
Text by the composer. Three acts. Presented by the Carl Rosa Opera Company.

1888 ## A. SULLIVAN: *The Yeomen of the Guard, or, The Merryman and his Maid*
3 October. London, Savoy
'A new and original opera'. Text by W. S. Gilbert. Two acts. The original manuscript score was bequeathed by the composer to the Royal College of Music.

1889 ## A. CELLIER: *Doris*
20 April. London, Lyric
Operetta. Text by B. C. Stephenson.

HENRI KOWALSKI: *Moustique*
2 July. Sydney, Opera House
Text by Marcus Clarke (author of *For the Term of his Natural Life*). Three acts.

STEPHEN PHILPOT: *Dante and Beatrice**
25 November. London, Brixton, Gresham Hall
Text by W. J. Miller. Three acts. Presented by the Carl Rosa Opera Company.

A. SULLIVAN: *The Gondoliers, or, The King of Barataria*
7 December. London, Savoy
'An entirely original comic opera'. Text by W. S. Gilbert. Two acts.

(1) After a few performances the title was changed to *Ruddigore*.

OSCAR F. TELGMANN: *Leo, the Royal Cadet*
Kingston (Ontario), Martin's Opera House
'An entirely new and original Canadian military opera'. Text by Cameron. Four acts.

The first production was under the patronage of the Royal Military College, Kingston. This operetta is reputed to have received 150 performances.

1890 **F. H. COWEN:** *Thorgrim**
22 April. Drury Lane
Text by Joseph Bennett. Four acts. Presented by the Carl Rosa Opera Company.

1891 **A. SULLIVAN:** *Ivanhoe**
31 January. London, Royal English Opera House
Text by Julian Sturgis. Three acts.

1892 **A. CELLIER:** *The Mountebanks*
4 January. London, Lyric
Comic opera. Text by W. S. Gilbert.

GEORGE D. FOX: *Nydia, the Blind Girl of Pompeii*
10 May. London, Crystal Palace
Text by the composer, after Bulwer Lytton's *The Last Days of Pompeii*.

I. DE LARA: *The Light of Asia**
11 June. Covent Garden
'Sacred legend'. English text by W. Beatty-Kingston, after the poem by Sir Edwin Arnold. Three acts.

This opera was originally composed as a cantata.

[HERMAN BEMBERG: *Elaine**
5 July. Covent Garden
French text by P. Ferrier, from Tennyson's *Idylls of the King*. Four acts.

This French opera by a French composer would not have been included here, had it not been for the fact that it was written for Dame Nellie Melba and seems to have been performed only in London and New York.]

GEORGE GROSSMITH: *Haste to the Wedding*
27 July. London, Criterion
Comic opera. Text by W. S. Gilbert.

A. SULLIVAN: *Haddon Hall*
24 September. London, Savoy
Light opera. Text by Sydney Grundy.

GRANVILLE BANTOCK: *Caedmar**
18 October. London, Crystal Palace
Text by the composer. One act.

L. EMIL BACH: *Irmengarda**
8 December. Covent Garden
Text by W. Beatty-Kingston.

1893 GUSTAV HOLST: *Lansdown Castle, or, The Sorcerer of Tewkesbury*
7 February. Cheltenham, Corn Exchange
Comic operetta. Text by Major A. C. Cunningham. Two acts.

A. G. THOMAS: *The Golden Web*
15 February. Liverpool, Royal Court
Text by F. Corder and B. C. Stephenson. Three acts. Presented by the Carl Rosa Opera Company.

ERNEST FORD: *Jane Annie, or, The Good Conduct Prize*
13 May. London, Savoy
Comic opera. Text by J. M. Barrie and A. Conan Doyle. Two acts.

I. DE LARA: *Amy Robsart**
20 July. Covent Garden
Text by A. H. G. Harris and F. E. Weatherley, after Sir Walter Scott's *Kenilworth*. Produced in a French translation by P. Milliet. Three acts.
  First production with the original English text, Grand Theatre, Croydon, 14 May 1920.

FREDERIC D'ERLANGER: *Jehan de Saintré**
1 August. Aix-les-Bains
French text by J. and P. Barbier. Two acts.
  Baron Frédéric d'Erlanger was born in Paris of a German father and American mother, but became a naturalised British subject.

A. SULLIVAN: *Utopia (Limited), or, The Flowers of Progress*
7 October. London, Savoy
'An original comic opera'. Text by W. S. Gilbert. Two acts.

F. H. COWEN: *Signa**
12 November. Milan, Teatro dal Verme
Text by G. A. à Beckett, H. A. Rudall, and F. E. Weatherley, after the novel by Ouida. Italian translation by G. A. Mazzucato. Three acts.
  Reduced to two acts (also in Italian) for the Covent Garden production on 30 June 1894.

1894 L. E. BACH: *The Lady of Longford**
21 July. Covent Garden
Text by A. H. G. Harris and F. E. Weatherley. Produced in an Italian translation by G. A. Mazzucato. One act.
  First production with the original English text, Drury Lane, 20 April 1896.

HAMISH MACCUNN: *Jeanie Deans**
15 November. Edinburgh, Lyceum
Text by J. Bennett, after Sir Walter Scott's *The Heart of Midlothian*. Four acts. Presented by the Carl Rosa Opera Company.

A. SULLIVAN: *The Chieftain*
12 December. London, Savoy

Operetta. Text by F. C. Burnand. A revised and enlarged version of *The Contrabandista* (1867).

1895 F. H. COWEN: *Harold, or, The Norman Conquest**
8 June. Covent Garden
Text by Sir Edward Malet. Three acts.

ALICK M. MACLEAN: *Petruccio**
25 July. Covent Garden
Text anonymous. One act.

J. PARRY: *Sylvia*
12 August. Cardiff
'Legendary grand opera'. Text by M. Parry. Three acts.

1896 C. V. STANFORD: *Shamus O'Brien*
2 March. London, Opéra Comique
Romantic comic opera. Text by G. H. Jessop, founded on the poem by Joseph Sheridan le Fanu. Two acts.

A. SULLIVAN: *The Grand Duke, or, The Statutory Duel*
7 March. London, Savoy
'A new and original comic opera'. Text by W. S. Gilbert. Two acts.

SIDNEY JONES: *The Geisha*
25 April. London, Daly's
Operetta. Text by O. Hall; lyrics by H. Greenbank. Two acts.

1897 A. C. MACKENZIE: *His Majesty, or, The Court of Vingolia*
20 February. London, Savoy
Comic opera. Text by F. C. Burnand and R. C. Lehmann. Two acts.

I. DE LARA: *Moina**
14 March. Monte Carlo
French text by L. Gallet. Two acts.

F. D'ERLANGER: *Inès Mendo**
10 July. Covent Garden
French text by P. Decourcelle and A. Liorat, after Prosper Mérimée. Three acts. (For this opera, D'Erlanger adopted the pseudonym of Frédéric Regnal.)

H. MACCUNN: *Diarmid**
23 October. Covent Garden
Text by the Marquis of Lorne (J. G. Campbell). Four acts. Presented by the Carl Rosa Opera Company.

1898 ETHEL SMYTH: *Fantasio**
24 May. Weimar
German Text by the composer, after Alfred de Musset. Two acts.

A. SULLIVAN: *The Beauty Stone*
28 May. London, Savoy
Romantic musical drama. Text by A. W. Pinero and J. W. Comyns Carr.

LEARMONT DRYSDALE: *The Red Spider*
25 July. Lowestoft
Comic opera. Text by S. Baring-Gould.

1899   I. DE LARA: *Messaline**
21 March. Monte Carlo
'A lyric tragedy'. French text by P. A. Silvestre and F. Morand. Four acts.

H. WALDO-WARNER: *Royal Vagrants*
27 October. London, Forest Gate, Earlham Hall
Comic operetta. 'A Story of Conscientious Objection'. Text by Cyril
Hurst. Two acts.

A. SULLIVAN: *The Rose of Persia, or, The Storyteller and
the Slave*
29 November. London, Savoy
Operetta. Text by Basil Hood.

1901   A. SULLIVAN and EDWARD GERMAN: *The Emerald
Isle*
27 April. London, Savoy
Comic opera. Text by Basil Hood.
    Sullivan failed to complete this score before his death.

C. V. STANFORD: *Much Ado About Nothing**
30 May. Covent Garden
Text by Julian Sturgis, after Shakespeare. Four acts.

1902   E. GERMAN: *Merrie England*
2 April. London, Savoy
Operetta. Text by Basil Hood. Two acts.

E. SMYTH: *Der Wald**
9 April. Berlin, Königliches Opernhaus
German text by the composer. Prologue, one act, epilogue.

HERBERT BUNNING: *Princesse Osra**
14 July. Covent Garden
French text by M. Bérenger, after a story by A. Hope. Three acts.

1903   LEGRAND HOWLAND: *Sarrona*
3 August. Bruges
English text by the composer. Prologue, one act.

COLIN MCALPIN: *The Cross and the Crescent**
22 September. Covent Garden
Anonymous text after F. Coppée's play *Pour la Couronne*. Four acts.
    This opera won the Charles Manners prize for the best English opera
and was presented by the Moody-Manners Company.

IVAN CARYLL: *The Duchess of Dantzic*
17 October. London, Lyceum
Operetta. Text by Henry Hamilton, from Sardou's *Madam Sans-Gêne*.
Three acts.

1904 FREDERICK DELIUS: *Koanga**
30 March. Elberfeld
English text by C. F. Keary, after G. W. Cable's novel *The Grandissimes*.
German version probably by the composer, or his wife Jelka. Prologue,
three acts, epilogue. This opera was composed by Delius in 1895–7.
First English performance at Covent Garden on 23 September 1935.

1905 A. C. MACKENZIE: *The Knights of the Road*
27 February. London, Palace
Operetta. Text by Henry A. Lytton.

AMHERST WEBBER: *Fiorella*
7 June. London, Waldorf
Original French text by V. Sardou and B. P. Gheusi. One act.
Revived (in English) at the Royal College of Music, 12 March 1928.

1906 I. DE LARA: *Sanga**
21 February. Nice
French text by E. Morand and P. de Choudens. Four acts.

NICHOLAS GATTY: *Greysteel, or, The Bearsarks Come
to Surnadale*
1 March. Sheffield
Text by R. Gatty (the composer's brother) after the Icelandic saga of
Gisli, the Soursop. One act. Presented by the Moody-Manners Company.
An expanded two-act version was performed at Sadler's Wells on 23
March 1938.

A. M. MACLEAN: *Die Liebesgeige**
Easter. Mayence
German text.

F. D'ERLANGER: *Tess**
10 April. Naples, San Carlo
Italian text by L. Illica, after Thomas Hardy's novel. Four acts.

E. SMYTH: *Strandrecht (The Wreckers)**
11 November. Leipzig
Original French text (*Les Naufrageurs*) by H. Brewster. German version
by H. Decker and J. Bernhoff. Three acts.
First stage production of the English version (translated by the composer and A. Strettell) at His Majesty's, 22 June 1909.

1907 F. DELIUS: *Romeo und Julia auf dem Dorfe (A Village
Romeo and Juliet)**
21 February. Berlin, Komische Oper
Text by the composer, after a story by Gottfried Keller. Prologue, six
scenes. This opera was composed by Delius in 1900–1.
First English performance at Covent Garden on 22 February 1910.

I. DE LARA: *Soléa*
19 December. Cologne
Original French text by J. Richepin and the composer. German translation by O. Neitzel. Four acts.

1908   JOSEPH HOLBROOKE: *The Stranger*
His Majesty's
Text by Walter E. Grogan. Two acts.

1909   EDWARD W. NAYLOR: *The Angelus**
27 January. Covent Garden
'Romantic opera'. Text by W. Thornely. Prologue, four acts. This opera was awarded the prize in Ricardi's English Opera Competition.

A. MACLEAN: *Maître Seiler*
August
Presented by the Moody-Manners Company.

J. HOLBROOKE: *Pierrot and Pierette*
11 November. His Majesty's
'Lyrical music drama'. Text by W. E. Grogan. Two scenes.

E. GERMAN: *Fallen Fairies*
15 December. London, Garrick
Light opera. Text by W. S. Gilbert.

N. GATTY: *Duke or Devil*
16 December. Manchester
'Farcical opera'. Text by I. Gatty. One act. Presented by the Moody-Manners Company.

1910   ROBERT O'DWYER: *Eithne*
16 May. Dublin
Erse text by T. O'Ceallaigh. Two acts. Played in Erse.

GEORGE CLUTSAM: *A Summer Night**
23 July. His Majesty's
Text by the composer. One act.

F. D'ERLANGER: *Noël**
28 December. Paris, Opéra Comique
French text by J. and P. Ferrier. Three acts.

1912   I. DE LARA: *Les Trois Masques**
24 February. Marseilles
French text by C. Méré. Produced in an Italian translation by Colautti. Four acts.
  First English performance at Greenock, near Glasgow, on 27 June 1919.

I. DE LARA: *Naïl**
22 April. Paris, Gaîté
French Text by J. Bois. Three acts.
  English version (translated by Edwin Evans) first performed at Covent Garden on 18 July 1919.

J. HOLBROOKE: *The Children of Don**
15 June. London Opera House
'A Cymric music drama'. Text by T. E. Ellis. Prologue, three acts. This opera was the first part of a trilogy called *The Cauldron of Annwn*.

G. CLUTSAM: *King Harlequin**
Berlin
'Music masque'. German translation by Rudolph Lothar. Four acts.

1913 RAYMOND RÔZE: *Joan of Arc*
1 November. Covent Garden
'Historical music drama'. Text by the composer. Prologue, three acts, and seven *Tableaux vivants*. Presented at the Raymond Rôze English Opera Season.

P. NAPIER MILES: *Westward Ho!**
4 December. London, Lyceum
Text by E. F. Benson. Prologue, three acts.

1914 A. C. MACKENZIE: *The Cricket on the Hearth*
6 June. London, Royal Academy of Music
Text by J. R. Sturgis, after Dickens. Three acts. The opera had been written some years previously and published in 1901.

MARSHALL HALL: *Stella*
8 June. London, Palladium
This opera was included in a variety bill at the Palladium. It was announced as being 'the first appearance of Australia in the operatic field'.

J. HOLBROOKE: *Dylan, Son of the Wave**
4 July. Drury Lane
Text by T. E. Ellis. Three acts. Part Two of *The Cauldron of Annwn*.

RUTLAND BOUGHTON: *The Immortal Hour**
26 August. Glastonbury, Somerset
'Music-drama'. Text adapted from the play and from poems of Fiona Macleod. Two acts.

1915 EDGAR L. BAINTON: *Oithona**
11 August. Glastonbury
Text by the composer, after Ossian. One act.

R. BOUGHTON: *Bethlehem**
28 December. Street, Somerset
Text adapted from the Coventry Nativity Play. Two acts.

1916   JOHN EDMUND BARKWORTH: *Romeo and Juliet**
7 January. Middlesbrough
Text by the composer, after Shakespeare. Four acts.

C. V. STANFORD: *The Critic, or, An Opera Rehearsed*
14 January. London, Shaftesbury
Text by L. C. James, after Sheridan. Two acts.

E. SMYTH: *The Boatswain's Mate*
28 January. London, Shaftesbury
Text by the composer, after the story by W. W. Jacobs. Two scenes.

R. BOUGHTON: *The Round Table**
14 August. Glastonbury
Music-drama. Text by Reginald Buckley and the composer. Three acts.
   This opera was the second of a cycle of five Arthurian music-dramas
composed by Boughton, consisting of *The Birth of Arthur* (1920), *The
Round Table* (1916), *The Lily Maid* (1934), *Galahad* and *Avalon*. The last
two operas of the cycle have so far not been produced.

CLARENCE RAYBOULD: *The Sumida River*
15 August: Glastonbury
Text by Marie Stopes, after the Japanese Noh play. One act.

G. HOLST: *Savitri**
5 December. London, Wellington Hall
Opera di camera. Text by the composer, after the Mahabharata. One act.
Written in 1908.

1919   F. DELIUS: *Fennimore und Gerda**
21 October. Frankfurt
German text by the composer, after J. P. Jacobsen's novel *Niels Lyhne*.
Nine scenes. This opera was composed by Delius in 1908–10. English
translation by Philip Heseltine. First produced in England by the Hammersmith Municipal Opera in 1968.

N. GATTY: *Prnce Ferelon, or, The Princess's Suitors**
27 November. London, Florence Ettlinger Opera School
'A musical extravaganza'. Text by the composer. One act.

1920   A. MACLEAN: *Quentin Durward*
13 January. Newcastle-upon-Tyne
Text by S. Ross, after Sir Walter Scott. Three acts. The opera had been
written many years previously and published in 1894. Presented by the
Carl Rosa Opera Company.

N. GATTY: *The Tempest**
17 April. London, Surrey
Text by R. Gatty, after Shakespeare. Three acts.

R. BOUGHTON: *The Birth of Arthur**
16 August. Glastonbury

Music-drama. Text by the composer and Reginald Buckley. Two acts. This was the prologue to the cycle of Arthurian music-dramas (see *The Round Table*, 1916).

REGINALD SOMERVILLE: *David Garrick*
9 December. Covent Garden
Text by the composer, from T. W. Robertson's play. Three acts. Presented by the Carl Rosa Company.

1921 **I. DE LARA:** *Les Trois Mousquetaires**
3 March. Cannes
French text by H. Cain and L. Payen, after Dumas. Six scenes.
  In English (translated by A. Kalisch), Newcastle-upon-Tyne, 2 May 1924.

CLIVE CAREY: *All Fools' Day*
29 August. Glastonbury
'A fantasy'. Text by T. M. Baretti. One act.

COLIN CAMPBELL: *Thais and Talmaae*
13 September. Manchester
Text by C. H. Bourne, after the novel by Anatole France. One act. Presented by the Carl Rosa Opera Company.

GEORGE D'ORLAY: *Le Chant Fatal*
7 December. Covent Garden
One act. Presented by the Carl Rosa Opera Company.

1922 **CYRIL ROOTHAM:** *The Two Sisters**
14 February. Cambridge, New Theatre
Text by Marjorie Fausset, founded on the ballad 'The Twa Sisters o' Binnorie'. Three acts.

RALPH VAUGHAN WILLIAMS: *The Shepherds of the Delectable Mountains**
11 July. London, Royal College of Music
Text after Bunyan. One act. Subsequently incorporated in *The Pilgrim's Progress* (1951).

R. BOUGHTON: *Alkestis**
26 August. Glastonbury
Music-drama. Text from Gilbert Murray's translation of the play by Euripides. Two acts.

ADRIAN WELLES BEECHAM: *The Merchant of Venice*
18 September. Brighton, Grand Theatre
Text from Shakespeare's play. Four acts.
  About ten years later Sir Adrian made an operatic setting of *Love's Labour's Lost*; but this was never produced.

1923 **G. HOLST:** *The Perfect Fool**
14 May. Covent Garden

Text by the composer. One act. Presented by the British National Opera Company.

E. SMYTH: *Fête Galante*
4 June. Birmingham
'A Dance-Dream'. Text by E. Shanks, after a story by Maurice Baring. One act. Presented by the British National Opera Company.

GEOFFREY PALMER: *Sruth Na Maoile (The Sea of Moyle)*
25 July. Dublin
Text by T. O'Ceallaigh (O'Kelly) after *The Children of Lir*.

HUBERT BATH: *Bubbles*
26 November. Belfast
Text from Lady Gregory's play, *Spreading the News*. One act. Presented by the Carl Rosa Opera Company.

C. ARMSTRONG GIBBS: *The Blue Peter*
11 December. London, Royal College of Music
Comic opera. Text by A. P. Herbert. One act.

1924   ### A. C. MACKENZIE: *The Eve of St John**
16 April. Liverpool
Text by Eleanor Farjeon. One act. Presented by the British National Opera Company.

LORD BERNERS: *Le Carrosse du Saint-Sacrement**
24 April. Paris, Théâtre des Champs-Elysées
French text, after the story by Prosper Mérimée. One act.

C. ARMSTRONG GIBBS: *Midsummer Madness*
3 July. Hammersmith, Lyric
Comic opera. Text by Clifford Bax. Three acts.

R. VAUGHAN WILLIAMS: *Hugh the Drover, or, Love in the Stocks**
4 July. London, Royal College of Music
'A romantic ballad opera'. Text by Harold Child. Two acts.

R. BOUGHTON: *The Queen of Cornwall**
21 August. Glastonbury
Music-drama. Text by Thomas Hardy. Two acts.

G. BANTOCK: *The Seal Woman**
27 September. Birmingham
Text by Fraser. Two acts.

P. NAPIER MILES: *Markheim**
13 October. Bristol, Victoria Rooms
'Dramatic sketch'. Text after the short story by Robert Louis Stevenson. One act.

P. NAPIER MILES: *Fire Flies**
13 October. Bristol, Victoria Rooms
'Comedy of masques'. Text by Julian Sturgis. One act.

1925 G. HOLST: *At the Boar's Head**
3 April. Manchester
'Musical interlude'. Text by the composer, after Shakespeare. One act.
Presented by the British National Opera Company.

C. V. STANFORD: *The Travelling Companion**
30 April. Liverpool
Text by Henry Newbolt, after Hans Andersen. Four acts.

CYRIL SCOTT: *Der Alchimist**
28 May. Essen
Text by the composer. German translation by Andreae. One act.

E. SMYTH: *Entente Cordiale*
22 July. London, Royal College of Music
'A post-war comedy'. Text by the composer. One act.

1926 MARTIN SHAW: *Mr Pepys*
11 February. Hampstead, Everyman
'Ballad opera'. Text by Clifford Bax. Three acts.

A. REYNOLDS: *The Policeman's Serenade**
10 April. Hammersmith, Lyric
'Comic opera'. Text by A. P. Herbert. One act. This opera, together with
Arne's *Thomas and Sally* (1760), formed part of the revue *Riverside
Nights*.

ERNEST BRYSON: *The Leper's Flute**
15 October. Glasgow
Text by Ian Colvin. Four acts. Presented by the British National Opera
Company.

1928 HEALEY WILLAN: *The Order of Good Cheer*
25 May. Quebec, Château Frontenac
'Ballad opera'. Text by Louvigny de Montigny, translated by J. Murray
Gibbon. The score was based on French Canadian folk songs.

M. SHAW: *Waterloo Leave*
12 November. Norwich, Maddermarket
'Ballad opera'. Text by Clifford Bax. Two acts.

1929 J. HOLBROOKE: *Bronwen**
1 February. Huddersfield
Text by T. E. Ellis. Three acts. Part III of *The Cauldron of Annwn*.
Presented by the Carl Rosa Opera Company. The score had been
completed early in 1920.

R. VAUGHAN WILLIAMS: *Sir John in Love**
21 March. London, Royal College of Music
Text by the composer, after Shakespeare. Four acts.

EUGENE GOOSSENS: *Judith**
25 June. Covent Garden
Text by Arnold Bennett. One act.

M. SHAW: *At the Sign of the Star**
6 December. London, Royal Albert Hall
Text by Barclay Baron. One act.

ALBERT COATES: *Samuel Pepys**
21 December. Munich
Text by Drury and Price. German translation by Meyerfeld. One act.

1930 **N. GATTY:** *King Alfred and the Cakes*
10 December. London, Royal College of Music
Text by Reginald Gatty. One act.

1931 **THOMAS F. DUNHILL:** *Tantivy Towers**
6 January. Hammersmith, Lyric
Comic opera. Text by A. P. Herbert. Three acts.

M. SHAW: *The Thorn of Avalon**
6 June. London, Crystal Palace
Text by Barclay Baron. Three acts.

WALTER LEIGH: *The Pride of the Regiment, or,*
Cashiered for his Country
19 September. Midhurst
Comic opera. Text by V. C. Clinton-Baddeley and Scobie Mackenzie.
Two acts.

ARTHUR BENJAMIN: *The Devil Take Her**
1 December. London, Royal College of Music
Text by Alan Collard. Prologue and one act.

1932 **A. REYNOLDS:** *Derby Day*
24 February. Hammersmith, Lyric
Comic opera. Text by A. P. Herbert. Three acts.

DONALD TOVEY: *The Bride of Dionysus**
25 April. Edinburgh
Text by R. C. Trevelyan. Three acts.

1933 **W. LEIGH:** *Jolly Roger, or, The Admiral's Daughter*
13 February. Manchester, Opera House
Comic opera. Text by Scobie Mackenzie and V. C. Clinton-Baddeley.
Three acts.

1934 **G. HOLST:** *The Wandering Scholar**
31 January. Liverpool, David Lewis Theatre

'Opera di camera'. Text by Clifford Bax, after an incident in Helen Waddell's *The Wandering Scholars*. One act.

LAWRANCE COLLINGWOOD: *Macbeth**
12 April. Sadler's Wells
Text by the composer, after Shakespeare. Three acts.

R. BOUGHTON: *The Lily Maid**
10 September. Stroud, Church Room
Music-drama. Text by the composer. Three acts.

GEORGE LLOYD: *Iernin**
6 November. Penzance
Text by W. Lloyd, the composer's father. Three acts.

1935   ### R. BOUGHTON: *The Ever Young**
9 September. Bath, the Pavilion
Music-drama. Text by the composer. Three acts.

1936   ### R. VAUGHAN WILLIAMS: *The Poisoned Kiss, or, The Empress and the Necromancer*
12 May. Cambridge, Arts Theatre
'A romantic extravaganza'. Text by Evelyn Sharp. Three acts.

M. SHAW: *Master Valiant**
June. London, Crystal Palace
Text by Barclay Baron. Three acts.

A. COATES: *Pickwick**
20 November. Covent Garden
Text by the composer, after Charles Dickens. Three acts.

ROGER QUILTER: *Julia*
3 December. Covent Garden
Light opera.

1937   ### W. B. MOONIE: *The Weird of Colbar**
22 March. Glasgow, Theatre Royal
Text by G. M. Reith. Three acts.

E. GOOSSENS: *Don Juan de Mañara**
24 June. Covent Garden
Text by Arnold Bennett. Four acts.

R. VAUGHAN WILLIAMS: *Riders to the Sea**
30 November. London, Royal College of Music
Text by J. M. Synge. One act.

1938   ### G. LLOYD: *The Serf**
20 October. Covent Garden
Text by W. Lloyd, the composer's father. Three acts.

1941   BENJAMIN BRITTEN: *Paul Bunyan*
4 May. New York, Columbia University
'Choral operetta'. Text by W. H. Auden. Prologue and two acts.
   First British production by the English Music Theatre Company at the
Maltings, Snape, 4 June 1976.

1942   H. WILLAN: *Transit through Fire**
8 March. Broadcast by C.B.C.
Radio opera. Text by John Coulter. One act. Commissioned by the
Canadian Broadcasting Corporation.

1944   E. L. BAINTON: *The Pearl Tree**
20 May. Sydney (New South Wales), Conservatorium of Music
Text by R. C. Trevelyan. Two acts.

1945   B. BRITTEN: *Peter Grimes**
7 June. Sadler's Wells
Text by Montagu Slater, after the poem by George Crabbe. Prologue and
three acts. Commissioned by the Koussevitzky Music Foundation. The
manuscript full score is in the Library of Congress, Washington, D.C.

1946   H. WILLAN: *Deirdre of the Sorrows**
20 April. Broadcast by C.B.C.
Text by John Coulter. Three acts. Commissioned by the Canadian
Broadcasting Corporation.
   The first stage performance took place on 2 April 1965 in the
MacMillan Theatre of the Edward Johnson Building, Toronto, when the
opera was presented by the Opera School of the Royal Conservatory of
Music.

INGLIS GUNDRY: *The Partisans**
28 May. London, St Pancras Town Hall
Text by the composer. One act.

B. BRITTEN: *The Rape of Lucretia**
12 July. Glyndebourne Opera House
Text by Ronald Duncan, after *Le Viol de Lucrèce* by André Obey.
Prologue, two acts, and epilogue.

1947   B. BRITTEN: *Albert Herring**
20 June. Glyndebourne Opera House
Comic opera. Text by Eric Crozier, after *Le Rosier de Madame Husson*
by Guy de Maupassant. Three acts. Presented by the English Opera
Group.

1948   ANTONY HOPKINS: *Lady Rohesia**
17 March. Sadler's Wells
'An operatic frolic' after one of Barham's *Ingoldsby Legends*. One act.

1949   A. BENJAMIN: *Primadonna**
23 February. London, Fortune
Text by Cedric Cliffe. One act.

I. GUNDRY: *Avon**
11 April. London, Scala
Text by the composer. Three acts.

B. BRITTEN: *The Little Sweep*
14 June. Aldeburgh, Jubilee Hall
Text by Eric Crozier. One act. This is the last act of the entertainment for
young people entitled *Let's Make an Opera!*

ARTHUR BLISS: *The Olympians*
29 September. Covent Garden
Text by J. B. Priestley. Three acts.

1950   BRIAN EASDALE: *The Corn King**
21 November. London, Paddington Hall Theatre
Text of this 'ritual opera' by Naomi Mitchison. Prologue and two acts.

1951   R. VAUGHAN WILLIAMS: *The Pilgrim's Progress**
26 April. Covent Garden
Text of this 'morality with music' by the composer after John Bunyan.
Prologue, four acts, epilogue.

G. LLOYD: *John Socman**
15 May. Bristol, Hippodrome
Text by W. Lloyd, the composer's father. Three acts. Presented by the
Carl Rosa Opera Company.

B. EASDALE: *The Sleeping Children**
9 July. Cheltenham, Opera House
Text by Tyrone Guthrie. Three acts. A chamber opera presented by the
English Opera Group.

A. HOPKINS: *The Man from Tuscany**
20 July. Canterbury, Chapter House
Text by Christopher Hassall. Two acts.

PETER TRANCHELL: *The Mayor of Casterbridge**
30 July. Cambridge, Arts Theatre
Text by Peter Bentley after the novel by Thomas Hardy. Three acts.

B. BRITTEN: *Billy Budd**
1 December. Covent Garden
Text by E. M. Forster and Eric Crozier, after the story by Herman
Melville. Prologue, four acts, epilogue: subsequently revised by the
composer (1960) into prologue, two acts, epilogue.

EGON WELLESZ: *Incognita**
5 December. Oxford, Town Hall
Text by Elizabeth Mackenzie, after the novel by William Congreve.
Three acts.

1952   GEOFFREY SHAW: *All at Sea*
12 May. London, Royal College of Music

Text of this ballad opera by Margaret Delamere and Sebastian Shaw.
Three acts.

1953   A. HOPKINS: *Scena*
1 *May*. B.B.C. Radio
An opera for broadcasting. Text by Patric Dickinson. One act. Commissioned by the B.B.C.

F. DELIUS: *Irmelin**
4 *May*. Oxford, New Theatre
Text by the composer. Three acts. This opera was composed by Delius in
1890–2. The Oxford performances were conducted by his friend Sir
Thomas Beecham.

B. BRITTEN: *Gloriana**
8 *June*. Covent Garden
Text by William Plomer. Three acts. Specially written for the Coronation
of Elizabeth II.

ANON: *Rab the Rhymer*
3 *July*. Aberdeen, Haddo House
Text of this ballad opera by Eric Crozier. The songs arranged by Isobel
Dunlop and Hans Oppenheim. Three acts.

J. ANTILL: *Endymion**
22 *July*. Sydney, Tivoli Theatre
This one-act opera was composed in 1924. Presented by the National
Opera of Australia.

ALAN BUSH: *Wat Tyler**
6 *September*. Leipzig, Opernhaus
Text by Nancy Bush, the composer's wife. Prologue and two acts.
German translation by Elfriede Brockmann-Neubauer and Max Zimmer-
ing.
    First English production at Sadler's Wells Theatre, 19 June 1974,
presented by the Keynote Opera Society.

I. GUNDRY: *The Tinners of Cornwall**
30 *September*. London, Rudolf Steiner Hall
Text by the composer. Three acts.

A. HUGHES: *Menna**
7 *November*. Cardiff
Text by Wyn Griffith. Three acts. Presented by the Welsh National Opera
Company.

A. HOPKINS: *Three's Company*
10 *November*. Intimate opera, London
Text by Michael Flanders. One act, three scenes.

1954   LENNOX BERKELEY: *A Dinner Engagement**
17 *June*. Aldeburgh, Jubilee Hall
Text by Paul Dehn. One act. A chamber opera presented by the English
Opera Group.

ERIC CHISHOLM: *Black Roses*
6 July. New York, Cherry Lane Theatre
One act.

B. BRITTEN: *The Turn of the Screw**
14 September. Venice, La Fenice
Text by Myfanwy Piper, after the story by Henry James. Prologue and two acts. A chamber opera presented by the English Opera Group.

L. BERKELEY: *Nelson**
22 September. Sadler's Wells
Text by Alan Pryce-Jones. Three acts.

WILLIAM WALTON: *Troilus and Cressida**
3 December. Covent Garden
Text by Christopher Hassall. Three acts. Originally commissioned by the B.B.C.

1955 ### MICHAEL TIPPETT: *The Midsummer Marriage**
27 January. Covent Garden
Text by the composer. Three acts. The manuscript full score (pencil) is in the British Library (Add. MS. 53, 771).

1956 ### A. BENJAMIN: *Mañana**
1 February. B.B.C. Television
Text by Caryl Brahms. One act. Commissioned by the B.B.C.

G. BUSH: *If the Cap Fits*
10 July. Cheltenham Opera House
Text by the composer, after Molière's *Les Précieuses Ridicules*. One act. Presented by Intimate Opera.

A. HOPKINS: *Ten O'Clock Call*
11 July. Cheltenham, Opera House
Text by Winifred Radford. One act. Presented by Intimate Opera.

I. GUNDRY: *The Logan Rock*
15 August. Porthcurno, Minack Theatre
Text of this 'comic opera' by the composer. Three acts.

L. BERKELEY: *Ruth**
2 October. London, Scala
Text by Eric Crozier. One act. A chamber opera presented by the English Opera Group.

A. BUSH: *Men of Blackmoor**
18 November. Weimar, Deutsches National Theater
Text by Nancy Bush. Three acts. German translation by Marianne Graefe.
  The English original first produced at the Town Hall, Oxford, by the Oxford University Opera Club, 30 November 1960.

MALCOLM ARNOLD: *The Open Window**
14 December. B.B.C. Television
Text by Sidney Gilliatt after Saki. One act. A chamber opera.

1957 JOAN TRIMBLE: *Blind Raftery**
22 May. B.B.C. Television
Text by Cedric Cliffe. One act. Commissioned by the B.B.C.

JOHN GARDNER: *The Moon and Sixpence**
24 May. Sadler's Wells
Text by Patrick Terry, after the novel by W. Somerset Maugham. Three acts.

A. BENJAMIN: *A Tale of Two Cities**
23 July. Sadler's Wells
Text by Cedric Cliffe, after the novel by Charles Dickens. Three acts. Presented by the New Opera Company.

1958 RICHARD ARNELL: *Love in Transit*
27 February. London, Guildhall School of Music
Text by Hal Burton. One act.

ANON: *Lord Bateman*
11 March. London, St Pancras Town Hall
Text of this ballad opera by Joan Sharp. Music arranged by Arnold Foster. Presented by the New Opera Company.

M. SAUNDERS: *The Little Beggars*
20 March. B.B.C. Television
Text of this 'ballad opera' by Caryl Brahms. One act. A chamber opera.

B. BRITTEN: *Noye's Fludde**
18 June. Orford Church, Suffolk
The Chester Miracle Play. One act. Presented by the English Opera Group.

THEA MUSGRAVE: *The Abbot of Drimock*
22 June. Park Lane Opera Group, Park Lane House, London
Text by Maurice Lindsay. One act, three scenes.

HUMPHREY SEARLE: *The Diary of a Madman**
3 October. Berlin Festival
Text by the composer, after the story by Gogol. One act. German translation by Hermann Scherchen. First English Production by the New Opera Company at Sadler's Wells, 26 April 1960.

1959 R. ARNELL: *The Petrified Princess*
5 May. B.B.C. Television
Text of this puppet opera by Bryan Guinness. One act. Commissioned by the B.B.C.

G. HALAHAN: *The Spur of the Moment*
17 June. B.B.C. Television
Text by Joe Mendoza. One act. Commissioned by the B.B.C.

PETER WISHART: *Two in the Bush*
23 June. Birmingham, Barber Institute
Text of this 'opera buffa' by D. J. Roberts. One act.

A. HOPKINS: *Hands across the Sky*
8 July. Cheltenham, Town Hall
Text by Gordon Snell. One act. Presented by Intimate Opera.

J. HOROVITZ: *Gentlemen's Island*
9 July. Cheltenham, Town Hall
Text by Gordon Snell. One act. Presented by Intimate Opera.

R. ARNELL: *Moonflowers*
23 July. Kentish Opera Group
Text by the composer. One act.

R. S. COKE: *The Cenci**
5 November. London, Scala
Text by the composer, after the play by Shelley. Three acts.

ELIZABETH MACONCHY: *The Sofa**
13 December. Sadler's Wells
Text by Ursula Vaughan Williams, after the novel by Crebillon (*fils*). One act. Presented by the New Opera Company (in a Workshop Production).

1960 **THOMAS EASTWOOD:** *Christopher Sly**
24 January. London, Royal Court
Chamber opera. Text by Ronald Duncan, after the play *The Taming of a Shrew*. Prologue, three acts, epilogue. Presented by the English Opera Group.

A. BLISS: *Tobias and the Angel**
19 May. B.B.C. Television
Text by Christopher Hassall. One act. Commissioned by the B.B.C.

F. BURT: *Volpone**
2 June. Stuttgart, Stadttheater
Text by the composer, after the play by Ben Jonson. Two acts.
   First English production by the New Opera Company at Sadler's Wells Theatre, 24 April 1961.

B. BRITTEN: *A Midsummer Night's Dream**
11 June. Aldeburgh, Jubilee Hall
Text by the composer and Peter Pears, after Shakespeare. Three acts. Presented by the English Opera Group.

P. WISHART: *The Captive*
29 June. Birmingham, Barber Institute
Text by Don Roberts. One act.

PHYLLIS TATE: *The Lodger**
14 July. London, Royal Academy of Music
Text by David Franklin, after the novel by Mrs Belloc-Lowndes. Two acts.

A. HUGHES: *Serch Yw'r Doctor*
1 August. Cardiff
Welsh text by Saunders Lewis, after Molière. Three acts. Presented by the Welsh National Opera Company at the National Eisteddfod.

HUGO COLE: *The Tunnel*
24 October. London, John Lewis Theatre
Text by the composer. Three acts.

1961 JOHN JOUBERT: *Silas Marner**
June. South African College of Music, University of Cape Town
Text by Rachel Trickett, after the novel by George Eliot. Three acts.
   First English production by the New Opera Company at Sadler's Wells Theatre, 1961.

RICHARD RODNEY BENNETT: *The Ledge**
11 September. Sadler's Wells
Text by Adrian Mitchell. One act.

DENIS ApIVOR: *Yerma**
17 December. B.B.C. Radio
Text by Montagu Slater, after the play by F. Garcia Lorca. One act. Commissioned by Sadler's Wells in 1954.

1962 A. SULLIVAN: *Engaged! or, Cheviot's Choice*
27 March. Bristol, Victoria Rooms
This pastiche comic opera (in three acts) was constructed by George Rowell and Kenneth Mobbs taking W. S. Gilbert's stage play *Engaged!* (1877) and adding music by Sullivan drawn from various lesser known scores of his, including *Thespis, The Sorcerer, Utopia (Limited), The Grand Duke*, and the overture *Di Ballo*.

M. TIPPETT: *King Priam**
29 May. Coventry, Coventry Theatre
Text by the composer. Three acts. Presented by the Covent Garden Opera Company. Commissioned by the Koussevitzky Music Foundation. Manuscript full scores are in the Library of Congress, Washington D.C. and the British Library (Egerton 3786).

P. TATE: *Dark Pilgrimage**
5 July. B.B.C. Television
Text by David Franklin. One act. Commissioned by the B.B.C.

E. MACONCHY: *The Departure**
16 December. Sadler's Wells
Text by Anne Ridler. One act. Presented by the New Opera Company.

BUXTON ORR: *The Wager**
16 December. Sadler's Wells
Text by Hamilton Johnston. One act. Presented by the New Opera Company.

EDWIN COLEMAN: *A Christmas Carol**
24 December. B.B.C. Television
Text by Margaret Burns Harris. Commissioned by the B.B.C.

1963 MALCOLM WILLIAMSON: *Our Man in Havana**
2 July. Sadler's Wells
Text by Sidney Gilliat, after the novel by Graham Greene. Three acts. Presented by Rostrum Ltd.

DANIEL JONES: *The Knife**
2 December. Sadler's Wells
Text by the composer. Two acts. Presented by the New Opera Company.

1964 H. SEARLE: *The Photo of the Colonel**
8 March. B.B.C. Third Programme
Text after Ionescu's story and play *The Killer*. Three acts. Commissioned by the B.B.C.

MICHAEL HURD: *Little Billy*
25 March. Newnham-on-Severn, Brightlands Prep School
Opera for children. Text by the composer after W. M. Thackeray. One act.

J. ECCLES: *Semele**
4 June. Oxford, Holywell Music Room
Opera. Text by William Congreve, adapted by Stoddart Lincoln. Three acts. Originally composed by Eccles in 1707 (*q.v.*), but not performed until 1964.

M. WILLIAMSON: *English Eccentrics**
11 June. Aldeburgh, Jubilee Hall
Chamber opera. Text by Geoffrey Dunn, after the book by Edith Sitwell. Two acts. Presented by the English Opera Group.

B. BRITTEN: *Curlew River**
13 June. Orford Church, Suffolk
Text for this 'parable for church performance' by William Plomer. One act. Presented by the English Opera Group.

JOHN TAVENER: *The Cappemakers*
14 June. Sussex Festival, Charleston Manor, Sussex.
Music drama in two acts, based on one of the York Mystery Plays.

PHILIP CANNON: *Morvoren**
15 July. London, Royal College of Music
Text by Maisie Radford. Two acts.

NICHOLAS MAW: *One Man Show**
12 November. London, Jeannetta Cochrane Theatre
Comic opera. Text by Arthur Jacobs, after Saki. Two acts. Commissioned by the London County Council. The score was revised in 1966.

A. BENJAMIN: *Tartuffe**
30 November. Sadler's Wells
Text by Cedric Cliffe, after the play by Molière. Two acts. Produced by the New Opera Company. (The vocal score was completed by the composer shortly before his death in 1960; and the orchestration was carried out by Alan Boustead.)

1965 **I. GUNDRY:** *The Prince of Coxcombs**
3 February. London, Morley College
Text by the composer after Vanburgh and Sheridan.

R. R. BENNETT: *The Mines of Sulphur**
24 February. Sadler's Wells
Text by Beverley Cross. Three acts. Commissioned by the Sadler's Wells Opera Company.
  For the revival at the Coliseum in 1973, the opera was reduced to two acts.

M. WILLIAMSON: *The Happy Prince*
22 May. Farnham Festival
Opera for children's and female voices. Text by the composer, after the story by Oscar Wilde. One act. Commissioned by Watney Mann Ltd.

CARL DAVIS: *The Arrangement**
30 May. B.B.C. Television
Text by Leo Lehman. One act. Commissioned by the B.B.C.

CHRISTOPHER WHELEN: *The Cancelling Dark**
5 December. B.B.C. Third Programme
Text by Vernon Scannell. One act. Commissioned by the B.B.C.

1966 **M. WILLIAMSON:** *Julius Caesar Jones**
4 January. London, Jeannetta Cochrane Theatre
Text by Geoffrey Dunn. Two acts. Commissioned by the Finchley Children's Music Group.

GRACE WILLIAMS: *The Parlour**
5 May. Cardiff
Text by the composer, after Guy de Maupassant's short story *En Famille*. One act. Presented by the Welsh National Opera Company.

B. BRITTEN: *The Burning Fiery Furnace**
9 June. Orford Church, Suffolk
Text for this 'second parable for church performance' by William Plomer. One act. Presented by the English Opera Group.

GORDON CROSSE: *Purgatory**
7 July. Cheltenham, Everyman Theatre

Text by W. B. Yeats. One act. Commissioned by the B.B.C. and the Cheltenham Festival Company. Presented by the New Opera Company.

P. TATE: *The What D'Ye Call It**
7 July. Cheltenham, Everyman Theatre
Text based on a Tragi-Comi-Pastoral Farce by John Gay, adapted by V. C. Clinton-Baddeley. One act. Commissioned by the Cheltenham Festival Company. Presented by the New Opera Company.

M. WILLIAMSON: *The Violins of St Jacques**
29 November. Sadler's Wells
Text by William Chappell, after the novel by Patrick Leigh Fermor. Three acts. Commissioned by the Sadler's Wells Trust and the Gulbenkian Foundation.

A. BUSH: *The Sugar Reapers**
11 December. Leipzig, Opera House
Text by Nancy Bush. German translation by Hans Michael Richter and Reinhard Geilert, with the German title Gayana Johnny. Two acts.

HERBERT CHAPPELL: *Mak the Sheep Stealer*
25 December. B.B.C. Television (Children's Programme)
Opera for children. Text by Don Taylor. One act. Commissioned by E.M.I.

1967 ## C. WHELEN: *Some Place of Darkness**
23 January. B.B.C. Television
Text by John Hopkins. One act. Commissioned by the B.B.C.

ALEXANDER GOEHR: *Arden Must Die**
5 March. Hamburg, State Opera
German text by Erich Fried, based on the same material as the play *Arden of Faversham*. English translation by Geoffrey Skelton. Two acts and epilogue. Commissioned by the Hamburg State Opera.
   The first English production was presented at Sadler's Wells Theatre on 17 April 1974 by the New Opera Company.

M. WILLIAMSON: *The Moonrakers**
22 April. Brighton
'Cassation for Audience and Orchestra'.[1] Text by the composer. One act. Commissioned by the Brighton Festival.

M. WILLIAMSON: *Dunstan and the Devil**
19 May. Cookham
Text by Geoffrey Dunn. One act. Commissioned by the Cookham Festival.

L. BERKELEY: *Castaway**
3 June. Aldeburgh, Jubilee Hall
Text by Paul Dehn. One act. Presented by the English Opera Group.

(1) This term was used by Malcolm Williamson to describe his 'miniature operas for audience-participation'.

W. WALTON: *The Bear**
3 June. Aldeburgh, Jubilee Hall
Text of this 'extravaganza' by Paul Dehn and the composer, after Anton Chehov. One act. Commissioned by the Serge Koussevitzky Music Foundation. Presented by the English Opera Group.

RICHARD STOKER: *Johnson Preserv'd**
4 July. London, St Pancras Town Hall
Text by Jill Watt. Three acts.

HAROLD NOBLE: *The Lake of Menteith**
13 August. B.B.C. Radio
Text by David Harris. One act. Commissioned by the B.B.C.

R. R. BENNETT: *A Penny for a Song**
31 October. Sadler's Wells
Text by Colin Graham, after the play by John Whiting. Two acts. Commissioned by the Sadler's Wells Opera Company.

T. MUSGRAVE: *The Decision**
30 November. Sadler's Wells
Text by Maurice Lindsay, based on a television play by Ken Taylor. Three acts. Presented by the New Opera Company.

1968   ## H. SEARLE: *Hamlet**
5 March. Hamburg State Opera
Text by the composer, after the play by Shakespeare. German translation by Hans Keller after A. W. von Schlegel. Three acts.
   First English production at Toronto, 12 February 1969.

ROBIN ORR: *Full Circle*
10 April. Perth
Text by Sydney Goodsir Smith. One act. Commissioned and produced by Scottish Opera.

M. WILLIAMSON: *Knights in Shining Armour**
29 April. Brighton
'Cassation for audience and piano'. Text by the composer. One act. Commissioned by the Brighton Festival.

M. WILLIAMSON: *The Snow Wolf**
30 April. Brighton
'Cassation for audience and piano'. Text by the composer. One act. Commissioned by the Brighton Festival.

NORMAN KAY: *The Rose Affair**
19 May. B.B.C. Television
Text ffrom the play by Alun Owen. One act. Commissioned by the B.B.C.

E. MACONCHY: *The Three Strangers**
5 June. Bishop Stortford College

Text adapted by the composer after Thomas Hardy's dramatisation of his short story of the same title. One act.

E. MACONCHY: *The Birds**
5 June. Bishop Stortford College
'Extravaganza'. Text adapted by the composer after Aristophanes. One act.

HARRISON BIRTWISTLE: *Punch and Judy**
8 June. Aldeburgh, Jubilee Hall
'A tragical comedy or a comical tragedy'. Text by Stephen Pruslin. One act. Commissioned and presented by the English Opera Group.

B. BRITTEN: *The Prodigal Son**
10 June. Ordford Church, Suffolk
Text for this 'third parable for church performance' by William Plomer. One act. Presented by the English Opera Group.

M. WILLIAMSON: *The Growing Castle**
13 August. Llandeilo, Dynevor Castle
Chamber opera. Text by the composer after *A Dream Play* by Strindberg. Two acts. Commissioned for the 1968 Dynevor Festival.

CHARLES CAMILLIERI: *Melita, or, A Cup Full of Tears*
28 November. Belfast, Aquinas Hall
Text by Ursula Vaughan Williams. One act.

1969   THOMAS WILSON: *The Charcoal Burner**
16 March. B.B.C. Radio
Text by Edwin Morgan. One act. Commissioned by the Broadcasting Council for Scotland.

A. HOPKINS: *Dr Musikus*
20 March. London, Arts Theatre
A children's opera. Text by the composer. One act. Presented by the Opera Players.

R. R. BENNETT: *All the King's Men!*
28 March. Coventry, Technical College
A children's opera. Text by Beverley Cross. One act.

T. EASTWOOD: *The Rebel**
4 April. B.B.C. Television
Text by Ronald Duncan. One act. Commissioned by the B.B.C.

H. BIRTWISTLE: *'Down by the Greenwood Side'**
8 May. Brighton, West Pier Pavilion
A dramatic pastoral. Text by Michael Nyman. One act. Commissioned by the Brighton Festival.

C. WHELEN: *Incident at Owl Creek**
26 May. B.B.C. Radio
Text by the composer, after the story by Ambrose Bierce. One act. Commissioned by the B.B.C. and produced in stereo.

J. JOUBERT: *Under Western Eyes**
29 May. London, St Pancras Town Hall
Text by Cedric Cliffe, after Conrad. Three acts. Presented by the New Opera Company.

G. CROSSE: *The Grace of Todd**
7 June. Aldeburgh, Jubilee Hall
Text by David Rudkin. One act. Presented by the English Opera Group.

DAVID BARLOW: *David and Bathsheba**
15 October. Newcastle upon Tyne, St Thomas's Church
Text by Ursula Vaughan Williams. One act.

A. HOPKINS: *Rich Man, Poor Man, Beggar Man, Saint**
18 October. Stroud, Holy Trinity Church
Text by G. David Nixon. Two acts. An opera written primarily for young people, both as singers and musicians.

RICHARD MORRIS: *Agamemnon**
25 November. Oxford, Playhouse
Text by Anthony Holden. Two acts. Presented by the Oxford University Opera Club. The opera was written when the composer and librettist were still undergraduates at Oxford.

F. BURT: *Barnstable**
30 November. Stuttgart, Stadttheater

M. WILLIAMSON: *Lucky Peter's Journey**
18 December. London, Coliseum
'A comedy with music'. Text by Edmund Tracey, after Strindberg. Three acts. Commissioned by the Sadler's Wells Trust and presented by the Sadler's Wells Opera Company.

MERVYN BURTCH: *The Selfish Giant**
25 December. B.B.C. Television, Wales
Text based on the story by Oscar Wilde. One act. Commissioned by the Guild for the Promotion of Welsh Music.

1970   **M. HURD:** *Mr Punch*
3 April. Göteborg, Götabergsskolan
Opera for children. Text by the composer. One act. Written for piano and percussion.

R. R. BENNETT: *Victory**
13 April. Covent Garden
Text by Beverley Cross, after the novel by Joseph Conrad. Three acts. Commissioned by the Friends of Covent Garden.

N. MAW: *The Rising of the Moon**
19 July. Glyndebourne Opera House
Operatic comedy. Text by Beverley Cross. Three acts.

A. BUSH: *Joe Hill: The Man Who Never Died**
29 September. Berlin, Deutsche Staatsoper
Text by Barrie Stavis. German translation by Marianne Gräfe-Petzoldt and Werner Otto. Two acts.

E. MACONCHY: *The Jesse Tree**
7 October. Dorchester Abbey, Oxon.
'A church opera or masque'. Text by Anne Ridler. One act. Commissioned for the Dorchester Abbey Festival.

I. GUNDRY: *The Prisoner Paul**
16 October. London, St Paul's, Covent Garden
Text adapted from the Acts of the Apostles by the composer. Two acts.

M. TIPPETT: *The Knot Garden**
2 December. Covent Garden
Text by the composer. Three acts. The manuscript (pencil) full score is in Northwestern University, Evanston.

1971 HAVERGAL BRIAN: *Agamemnon**
January. London, St John's, Smith Square
This one-act opera was composed in 1957; and it was first heard at a concert performance (as above) to celebrate the composer's 95th birthday.

ALAN RIDOUT: *The Pardoner's Tale**
1 April. Canterbury, Marlowe Theatre
Text by Norman Platt, after Chaucer. One act. Commissioned by Regional Opera Trust.

ANTHONY GILBERT: *The Scene-Machine**
4 April. Kassel, State Theatre
Text by George Macbeth. German translation (*Das Popgebeuer*) by Lutz and Irene Liebelt. One act. Commissioned by the Kassel State Theatre.
First English production by the New Opera Company at Sadler's Wells Theatre on 1 March 1972.

B. BRITTEN: *Owen Wingrave**
16 May. B.B.C. Television
Text by Myfanwy Piper, after the story by Henry James. Two acts. Commissioned by the B.B.C.
First stage performance, Covent Garden, 10 May 1973.

P. WISHART: *The Clandestine Marriage**
8 June. London, Guildhall School of Music
Text by Don Roberts, after the play by George Colman and David Garrick. Three acts. Commissioned by the Guildhall School of Music.

M. WILLIAMSON: *Genesis**
June. North Carolina

'Cassation for audience and instruments'. Text by the composer. One act. Commissioned for the 1971 Children's Choir Camp in the Diocese of Western North Carolina, U.S.A.

M. WILLIAMSON: *The Stone Wall**
18 September. London, Royal Albert Hall
'Cassation for audience and orchestra'. Text by the composer. One act. Commissioned by the B.B.C. for the Henry Wood Promenade Concerts.

M. HURD: *The Widow of Ephesus**
23 October. Stroud, Subscription Rooms
Chamber opera. Text by David Hughes and the composer. One act.

STEPHEN OLIVER: *The Duchess of Malfi**
23 November. Oxford, Playhouse
Text adapted by the composer from the play by John Webster. Three acts. Presented by the Oxford University Opera Club.

BARRY CONYNGHAM: *Edward John Eyre*
University of New South Wales Opera, Australia
Text by the composer and Meredith Oakes, after Geoffrey Dutton's biography of Eyre. One act.

1972　　ELISABETH LUTYENS: *Time Off? Not a Ghost of a Chance!*
1 March. Sadler's Wells
'A charade in four scenes with three interruptions'. Text by the composer. Presented by the New Opera Company.

M. WILLIAMSON: *The Red Sea**
14 April. Dartington College of Arts, Devon
Opera for children. Text by the composer. One act. Commissioned by the Dartington Arts Society.

J. GARDNER: *The Visitors**
7 June. Aldeburgh, Jubilee Hall
Text by John Ormerod Greenwood. Three acts. Presented by the English Opera Group.

PETER MAXWELL DAVIES: *Taverner**
12 July. Covent Garden
Text by the composer. Two acts.

C. WHELEN: *The Findings**
16 July. B.B.C. Radio 3
Text by the composer. One act. Commissioned by the B.B.C.

GEORGE DREYFUS: *Garni Sands**
12 August. Sydney, University of New South Wales
Text by Frank Kellaway. With eight singers and fifteen instrumentalists, this would seem to come into the category of chamber opera. It was hailed by the Australian press as 'the first full-length opera with a 100% Australian content to be staged in Australia for at least half a century'.

GEOFFREY BUSH: *Lord Arthur Savile's Crime**
5 December. London, Guildhall School of Music
Text by the composer, after the story by Oscar Wilde. One act.

JOHN PURSER: *The Bell**
27 December. B.B.C. Radio
Radio opera. Text by the composer's father, J. W. R. Purser. One act. A joint commission of B.B.C. Scotland and the Scottish Broadcasting Council.

1973 J. JOUBERT: *The Prisoner*
14 March. Queen Elizabeth's School, Barnet
Text by Stephen Tunnicliffe. Two acts. Commissioned by Queen Elizabeth's School in celebration of its fourth centenary.

E. LUTYENS: *Infidelio**
17 April. Sadler's Wells
Text by the composer. One act. Composed in 1953. Presented by the New Opera Company.

CHARLES WILSON: *The Summoning of Everyman**
April. Dalhousie University, Halifax, Nova Scotia
Text adapted by Eugene Benson after the medieval morality play. One act.

B. BRITTEN: *Death in Venice**
16 June. Snape, Maltings
Text by Myfanwy Piper, after the story by Thomas Mann. Two acts. Presented by the English Opera Group.

C. WILSON: *Héloise and Abélard**
September. Toronto, O'Keefe Centre
Text by Eugene Benson. Three acts. Commissioned and presented by the Canadian Opera Company.

C. WILSON: *The Selfish Giant**
December. Toronto, St Lawrence Centre
Opera for children. Text adapted by the composer from the story by Oscar Wilde. One act. Commissioned and presented by the Canadian Children's Opera Chorus.

1974 P. WISHART: *Clytemnestra**
13 February. London, Collegiate Theatre, University College
Text by Don Roberts. Two acts.

G. CROSSE: *The Story of Vasco**
13 March. London, Coliseum
Libretto based on an English version by Ted Hughes of the play *Histoire de Vasco* by Georges Schehadé. Three acts. Commissioned and presented by the Sadler's Wells Opera.

IAIN HAMILTON: *The Catiline Conspiracy**
16 March. Stirling, McRobert Centre

Text by the composer. Two acts. Commissioned and presented by Scottish Opera.

ALUN HODDINOTT: *The Beach of Falesa**
26 March. Cardiff, New Theatre
Text by Glyn Jones, after the story by Robert Louis Stevenson. Three acts. Presented by the Welsh National Opera.

T. MUSGRAVE: *The Voice of Ariadne**
11 June. Aldeburgh, Jubilee Hall
Text by Amalia Elguera, after Henry James's story *The Last of the Valerii*.

1975   G. CROSSE: *Potter Thompson*
9 January. London, Church of St Mary Magdalene, Munster Square
Music drama for children. Text by Alan Garner. One act.

R. ORR: *Hermiston**
27 August. Edinburgh, King's Theatre
Text by Bill Bryden, after *Weir of Hermiston* by Robert Louis Stevenson. Three acts. Commissioned and presented by Scottish Opera.

E. MACONCHY: *The King of the Golden River**
29 October. University Church, St Mary's, Oxford
A music drama for children. Text by Anne Ridler, after *The King of the Golden River* by John Ruskin. One act.

1976   G. BUSH: *The Equation*
6 February. B.B.C. Radio 3

EDWARD HARPER: *Fanny Robin*
8 February. B.B.C. Radio 3

S. OLIVER: *Tom Jones*
17 April. Newcastle upon Tyne, University Theatre
Text by the composer. Commissioned and presented by the English Music Theatre Company.

THOMAS WILSON: *The Confessions of a Justified Sinner**
17 June. York, Theatre Royal
Text by John Currie, after the story by James Hogg. Three acts. Commissioned and presented by Scottish Opera.

1977   M. TIPPETT: *The Ice Break**
7 July. Covent Garden
Text by the composer. Three acts.

T. MUSGRAVE: *Mary, Queen of Scots*
6 September, Edinburgh Festival, King's Theatre.
Text by the composer, based on *Moray*, play by Amalia Elguera. Commissioned by Scottish Opera.

DAVID BLADE: *Toussaint l'Ouverture, or, The Aristocracy of the Skin*
29 September. Coliseum
Text by Tony Ward. Commissioned by the Gulbenkian Foundation and presented by the English National Opera. Three acts.

1978 MAXWELL-DAVIES: *The Two Fiddlers*
16 June. Kirkwall Grammar School, Kirkwall, Orkney
Opera for children. Text by the composer.

1979 J. TAVENER: *Thérèse*
1 October. Royal Opera House, Covent Garden
Text by Gerald McLarnon. One act.

1980 DAVID SELWYN: *The Rocking Stone*
23 February. Bristol Grammar School.
Text by the composer. Two acts.

ANDREW WILSON DIXON: *Errors*
21 June. Leicester University at Haymarket Studio, Leicester
Text by Roger Warren from Shakespeare's *Comedy of Errors*.

P. MAXWELL-DAVIES: *The Lighthouse*
2nd September. Edinburgh
Text by the composer. Commissioned by the Edinburgh International Festival. Prologue and one main act.

Addenda

Index to Titles

Where there are titles of the same name, the composer's name has been specified.
Alternative titles have not been given.

Published contemporaneously with this volume

A HISTORY OF ENGLISH OPERA
Eric Walter White
Faber and Faber £30.00

Eric Walter White traces the history and development of English opera from its beginnings in the sixteenth century in incidental music, farce jigs, and court masques, right up to the post-war operatic renaissance as evidenced in the works of Benjamin Britten and Michael Tippett.

The author devotes himself not only to the composers and the librettists, but also to how their operas have been staged, to the finance and administration of the theatres, and to public and critical reaction. Over a dozen composers are discussed at length, including Locke, Purcell, Handel, Arne, Dibdin, Storace, Balfe, Sullivan, Delius, Smyth, Boughton, Britten and Tippett.

The book begins with an account of the birth of opera in Italy and its influence on English composers. The first part covers the tentative beginnings in the sixteenth and seventeenth centuries, and the second culminates in the magnificent achievements of Purcell. The third part is largely devoted to the great age of Handel and to the rise of the popular ballad opera. The fourth part begins with the romantic movement, before turning to Balfe and the vogue for Gilbert and Sullivan. The fifth and final part is especially concerned with the up-to-date history of such theatres as Sadler's Wells and Covent Garden, and with the remarkable developments that have caught the imagination of the entire musical world since *Peter Grimes* burst upon the scene in 1946.

Eric Walter White has devoted a lifetime's research to this book, which will surely be regarded as the definitive study of its subject.

THE SOCIETY FOR THEATRE RESEARCH

provides a meeting point for all those—scholars, research workers, actors, producers and theatregoers—who are interested in its history and technique. Founded in 1948, the Society now occupies an established and authoritative position in the field of British theatre history, and is especially concerned to link this to modern theatre practice.

An Annual Publication (of which *A Register of First Performances of English Operas* is one) is sent free to all members, and members may obtain past publications of the Society at a price lower than the regular published price.

Theatre Notebook, an illustrated journal devoted to the history of the British theatre, is published three times a year, and this, too, is supplied free to members. Articles range over all periods of British theatre, from the medieval to the twentieth century, and over all forms of theatrical entertainment, including opera and ballet.

Monthly meetings are held in London during the winter, with lectures on a wide range of theatre topics. An Annual Public Lecture is given, usually in May.

The Society welcomes enquiries on aspects of theatre history that cannot be answered from normal published sources. It cannot undertake research on behalf of its members but it can sometimes put enquirers in touch with other researchers in the same field.

The Society welcomes applications for membership, both individual and corporate. Details may be obtained from the Hon. Secretary at 77 Kinnerton Street, London SW1X 8ED.